What's the Issue?

Biblioguidance for children that opens doors!

by DeDe Coffman

Publisher—

Educational Media Corporation®
P.O. Box 21311
Minneapolis, MN 55421-0311

(763) 781-0088 or (800) 966-3382

www.**educationalmedia**.com

Production editor—

Don L. Sorenson

Graphic design—

Earl Sorenson

Dedication

I dedicate this book to my maternal and parental grandparents who always made me feel like I could "move mountains." Thanks for showing me, through your living example, the exact fruit that all children need: peace, joy, and love—a never-ending agape love!

Acknowledgments

To my husband, Marty, for always encouraging me to pursue my dreams and for showing me what giving of self really means. You are the greatest!

To my children, Bridge and Brooks, for loving me when I'm not lovable and allowing me to not only be a mom to them, but a friend to many other children.

To my dad, Tommy, for financially helping me with the book, so that I could reach more children than I ever thought possible with this "little idea of mine." You are the most giving man I know!

To my pastors, Keith and Sheila, and friends at Celebration Covenant Church, you will never know how much you inspire me to be all I can be through Christ. Thank you for teaching me that "I can't hit if I don't swing."

To Mr. Tucker, Mrs. Harris, Mr. Ulibari, Mr. Pierson, and Mr. Bell for the great beginnings on this educational journey. Thanks for sharing your knowledge and patience with me.

To Mr. Watkins, and the administrators and staff at Prosper ISD, for going above and beyond in serving children. You truly put children first.

For children I have had the honor of working with in the past, you have all touched my life in ways you will never know. I know more about this journey because of you!

To God, for giving me every gift that I have and extending His Grace to cover for the ones I don't have. He truly is the Lover of my Soul. May all I do glorify Him.

Table of Contents

"Few children learn to read books by themselves. Someone has to lure them into the wonderful world of the written word; someone has to show them the way."

—Orville Prescott

©2005 Educational Media Corporation© Box 21311, Minneapolis, MN 55421-0311

About the Author

Hi!. I am DeDe Coffman, M.Ed., a diverse educational veteran in the North Texas area. During the last nine years in the public school setting, I have worked as a secondary classroom teacher (history, government/economics, language arts, physical education, special education), coach, and currently as an elementary guidance counselor in Prosper, Texas. I obtained my undergraduate degree in Kinesiology from the University of North Texas and my master's degree in Education from Dallas Baptist University. I am the founding person of Lifesavers, a networking group for small school counselors in the North Texas area and a certified Second Step Trainer (a national anti-violence curriculum). I also was a featured session speaker at the Texas Education Agency's state convention in 2004. I am currently a member of the Texas Counselor's Association.

The experiences and opportunities with children that my educational journey has provided are priceless. They have forced me to find my passion in life and to begin "thinking out of the box" for ways to reach the WHOLE child. I recently started "What's the Issue? Educational Resources" to help parents, educators, and other childcare professionals creatively reach and teach all children, not only academically, but socially and emotionally as well. For more information on consulting, trainings, speaking or continuing education, please email mdcoffman@sbcglobal.net or call (214) 578.5784. Everyday we get the honor of planting seeds, watching beautiful minds grow, and seeing children find wings to fly. I have decided that Winston Churchill was right, "We make a living by what we get. We make a life by what we give."

If you are looking for a SIMPLE way to make a difference in the lives of children, you don't have to look any further. Books are powerful vehicles of communication. In this book, you will find research into biblioguidance, as well as practical, ready-to-go information on common childhood issues, such as worry, anger, goal-setting, friendships, and manners that will help you to get into the "heart" of a child. If you need a boost for your school that enhances social-emotional learning, while getting students to read, then this is for you. Or, if you are a parent who wants to see the relationship between you and your children go to new levels as they GROW through life's processes, then I encourage you to look no further. Put this communication tool to work for your family. Life is never about "When I get there, I am going to.... It's about "Because I have become more today, I will enjoy the benefits of tomorrow."

For Schools

"It's not how you live, it's whose life you change in the wake of yours."
—Source unknown

What's the Issue?

Counseling children seems to be an increasingly difficult task. Mental health and school professionals who work with children, whether in private or public settings, are under pressure to work quickly and creatively, but often with limited resources. Bibliotherapy, referred to as biblioguidance in this book, is a very productive and non-threatening way to reach more children in the public school setting. Using books, along with discussions and activities to help children grow socially and emotionally, is vital in our fast-paced society. No longer can we just teach academics in the school setting. Children also must learn how to interact in society, which starts with understanding self. One of the largest parts of self is emotions. Most counselor-student ratios are so great that rarely are all needy children comforted. There just is not enough time and people to go around; however, a simple biblioguidance program can help. In this program, children or parents can voluntarily sign up for small group reading clubs that meet to discuss issues found in children's books. It becomes more of a fun, personal growth, extracurricular activity to join, rather than a "counseling" type situation. With the new "No Child Left Behind" Act breathing down our necks, it also encourages reading! It is a proactive concept to combining reading and social-emotional learning.

I have found that children love the chance to read and apply the information from books to their personal lives. All children find some hope in every topic covered because they are relevant and real to their lives. As educators, we have been taught to expand upon prior learning experiences. That is easily accomplished by connecting characters in books to children's lives. The group situation also adds much to the discussions as peers share personal stories, questions, and information. Parents have also found it to be a great tool for enhancing their relationships with their children. A second grade parent told me, "After discussing the questions on worry, I found out what it is that my daughter does worry about and we talked through it extensively. It amazed me that, as her mother, I never knew she worried about these things."

This book is meant to serve as a comprehensive guide for schools trying to make a positive difference in the lives of children. By incorporating children's literature into an understanding and knowledge of how to effectively help children, a biblioguidance program can comfort children facing some of the most common issues of today.

DeDe Coffman

The goal of this book is to:

➤ Give a brief research overview of biblioguidance

➤ Provide examples of monthly topics with materials to use

➤ Provide set up information and allow for creative, personalized organization of the program

What's the Issue? is a practical, step-by-step guide to leading effective biblioguidance programs for children. It is designed for counselors, parents, and other educational workers interested in helping young people develop the skills, attitudes, and beliefs needed for success in school and life. President Franklin Roosevelt once said, "We can not prepare the future for our children, but we can prepare our children for the future."

In the beginning of this book, I give you a little background information on my experiences, as well as research information and an explanation of the program I have started. The next few sections of the book are divided into topics. Basically, I recommend two children's books for each topic, one of which is bilingual. Each topic has enough information included with it to conduct a biblioguidance session. Each session contains the following:

✔ Display for bulletin boards, and so forth.

✔ Bilingual discussion page to send home with students who have signed up in advance of the meeting.

✔ Meeting agenda.

✔ Procedures and copies of activities and lessons.

✔ Bilingual letters to send home to parents after the meeting about the topic.

In addition, there is information on setting the program up and bilingual sample forms, letters, memos, and other documents to use in implementation.

It is my hope that these pages will not only be useful tools for working with children and families, but that they will stimulate new ways for you to look at problems and find solutions. As you complete looking at this book, may you never forget to keep your own battery charged so you can be of service to others and so you are strategically in a place to make a difference in thousands of lives—one-at-a-time.

(*Feel free to make copies of letters and other school-home communication, if needed. For additional copies of* **What's the Issue?** *for your staff or parents, please contact www.educationalmedia.com.*)

DeDe Coffman

For Parents

"Sometimes the heart sees what is invisible to the eye."

—H. Jackson Brown, Jr.

When starting this book, my vision was limited to the school setting because that is where I was using biblioguidance. I had been using it at home with my own children when at an impasse. I had even suggested a few books to friends. I didn't pay attention to all the comments that parents were making about how the club was changing parent-child relationships at home. I mean, I was always glad to hear that parents were supporting me instead of "the alternative," but it wasn't until after the book went to the publishers that I thought, "DeDe, you've forgotten all about the most important part of the equation—the parents." (This could also be a great social-emotional curriculum for home school children). By using the appropriate book, inquisitive questioning, and unconditional positive regard as us counselors call it, or otherwise known as "empathy," parents can become the "professionals on duty" by using biblioguidance. Research is provided in one of the chapters so that you, as a parent, can fully understand how books can serve to guide children in expressing themselves. Over and over again, I have heard from parents about the increased communication at home because of book club. Machelle, a second grade parent says, "As an educator and parent, I am so excited that the book club is addressing these various issues. While I feel my daughter and I have good communication skills, it wasn't until the book club addressed these specific topics that I realized how she felt about the issues of self-esteem, friendship, and problem-solving. It has been a good way for us to focus on specific issues affecting her everyday."

In a healthy family, the parent is the number one teacher and guide. In an unhealthy family, the children bring themselves up the best they can. Perfect parenting is a myth; however, responsible parenting is not. Parents are people. They are human. They make mistakes; however, by being a part of your child's inner thoughts, you can let them know that you care and are willing to be there for them. You get to hear their heart! Isn't that all that really matters in any relationship? By using the suggested books and discussion pages in this book as a springboard, I believe that you can go to a new level of intimacy with your child and help them grow up feeling like they matter. Children will be affirmed and made to feel that they are worthy which is the bottom level of human need according to famed psychologist Abraham Maslow.

The bonds that are established between parent and child through biblioguidance can be quite strong. Jennifer, the parent of a first grade boy, says, "A special bond develops as you read the books together and go over the discussion questions." You, as a parent, are the most important person in your child's life. More than anything else your child wants to know how you feel and in turn share how he/she feels. What a wonderful by-product of reading and discussing a book.

The sensitive exploration of common childhood problems that takes place through parents using biblioguidance brings restoration and transformation. When my own son was six-months-old, his pediatrician wrote a prescription for reading. It said, "Read to child once daily." The medical field has long been avid supporters of the positive affects of reading between parent and child.

There are many more sophisticated techniques and recommendations out there on communicating and bonding with your child. I offer biblioguidance and this book as a simple way, in an often too busy world, to make a difference in your child's life. Use it as you wish, but know that the benefits of this type of guidance in your family are endless.

Books are treasure chests full of wisdom that can strengthen, not only the intra-personal relationship, but the interpersonal as well. When your child is worried, pull out *What's the Issue?* flip to the worry section, find the book, and let the character work as a vehicle of communication between you and your child. Use the activities as they are or tweak them for your specific purposes.

Keith Craft, leadership strategist and my pastor, believes that all of life is a process and that we "grow" through things instead of "go" through them. All of life IS a process and, by using this book as a model, you and your child WILL grow together! You will begin to see your children and their struggles with fresh eyes, and you may even stumble onto a whole new, wonderful dimension to their personalities that escaped you before. While navigating some of life's toughest childhood issues, through the process of biblioguidance, your children will find solace and love. (www.leadershipshapers.com)

My Story

"Life isn't about finding yourself, life is about creating yourself."
—George Bernard Shaw

This book has been in the making many years. I just didn't know it at the time. Hindsight truly is 20/20. When I graduated from college in 1996, I never dreamed that I would ever have the creativity, stamina, or patience to work with kids, let alone inspire them to be all they can be. Yes, someday I would have my own to raise and mold perfectly (what a dream), but never hundreds of others from all "walks of life." My thoughts were that "I was going to DO SOMETHING with my life" and at the same time make a lot of money. Oh, the thoughts of a 21-year-old.

Ringgggg.... Ringgggg. "Hello."

"Hello, DeDe, How are you doing today? This is W.R. Tucker."

"Hey W.R., I'm fine!" (wondering why he's calling) "You want me to do what? Are you serious? I don't think...."

That was how the conversation went or something real close to it. Mr. Tucker, one of my dad's friends, thought I needed to try coaching. I guess he was desperate. He said he had seen me play ball and he thought I would be a great girls' coach... and I needed a job. So, in a small speck of the road in North Texas, I began my first coaching/teaching job at Prairie Valley School, which, in 2004, was honored as a national Blue Ribbon School. All seventy plus kids (yes, that's K-12) were in one building and, if you blinked as you drove by the school, you might miss it. As small as it was, I couldn't have picked a better place, or more supportive environment, in which to start figuring out what was truly important in life. Mr. Tucker, a retired (two times over), educational veteran, made sure that I learned things the right way, but also allowed me enough room to wiggle around and make some things my own—like the basketball program. I found a little success with that and, well, as the old saying goes, "I was hooked." Connecting with those girls was one of the best things I could have ever done. It provided just the right amount of human connection to help me see that working with kids was going to define my life.

After deciding to start a family of my own, I gave up coaching, only to go back several times. That was one of those things that I just couldn't get out of my system. So, whether I was teaching a P.E. class in Saint Jo, coaching (again) in Nocona, or driving two hours round trip to Krum (only to be with freshman history students), the experiences and opportunities my educational journey have provided are priceless (I think I could do some of those Mastercard commercials). All of those countless hours spent with kids of all ages from all different backgrounds helped me to find passion in my life and forced me to "think out of the box" for ways to reach them. Life soon found me in Prosper, Texas where the name of the town pretty much describes the surroundings. Having gotten out of the classroom in Prosper, I now have the opportunity to design and implement creative programs to facilitate kids socially and emotionally to reach their full potential. I am in a place that is on the "cutting edge" of defining what it means to teach the WHOLE child. I continue to learn from working under some of the best administrators in the business, that schools may be the only stable hand that a child can hold. The education system does work if we put the kids first!

So here I am writing this book—DOING SOMETHING with my life. Have I reached completion yet? What a joke! The closer I get to finding life's answers, the more I realize how much I don't know. I will just continue to work in the trenches, sharing along the way. Do I make a lot of money? Well, what does that really have to do with it anyway? Each and every day I get the honor of planting seeds, watching beautiful minds grow, and seeing children find wings to fly. I have decided that Winston Churchill was right, "We make a living by what we get. We make a life by what we give."

The Research

"We cannot teach people anything; we can only help them discover it within them- selves."

—Galileo Galilei

History

Bibliotherapy has been around a long time. For as far back as Plato, people have been concerned with molding minds through literature. Isn't that what reading does? The prevailing effects of reading have been known since ancient times, but it was only in the early 1900s that a precise term was created for the use of books to affect a change in a person's thinking or behavior. Samuel Crothers conversed about a technique of recommending books to patients who needed insight into their problems; he identified the technique as "bibliotherapy" (Crothers, 1916, p. 291). Other definitions included "guided reading or written materials in gaining understanding or solving problems relevant to a person's therapeutic needs" (Riordan and Wilson, 1989, p. 506). These uses of bibliotherapy were originally restricted to hospitals during WWI. By 1940, its use had extended to a multitude of situations, and in 1946 bibliotherapy was first used with children (Agnes, 1946, pp. 8-16).

Bibliotherapy underwent many changes throughout the twentieth century. By 1975, Henry Olsen began discussing, in detail, copious real-world tribulations challenging children, and argued that bibliotherapy was proper in the current world because it permitted kids a safe way of dealing with impasses. "Through bibliotherapy," he stated, "children have an opportunity to identify, to compensate, and to relive in a controlled manner a problem that they are aware of" (Olsen, 1975, p. 425). He associated bibliotherapy with the prevention of a disease, and advocated that, because books help children develop their self-concepts, they will be better adjusted to trying situations in the future (Olsen, 1975, p. 425).

What is it?

Bibliotherapy generally refers to the use of literature to help people cope with emotional problems, mental illness, or changes in their lives (Pardeck, 1994), or to produce affective change and promote personality growth and development (Lenkowsky, 1987; Adderholdt-Elliott & Eller, 1989). With children, bibliotherapy gives the okay to children that it is normal to talk about this, and together we can come up with a solution. This type of therapy is useful because it allows children to step back from their problems and experience them from objective viewpoints. It offers a safe place to investigate feelings and is a nonthreatening way to raise sensitive subjects. It can also be used proactively to anticipate issues before they are "fires to put out."

The simple act of reading a story is not bibliotherapy. Discussions, activities and illustrations must be incorporated for the issue to be adequately worked through. It is a conversation starter, not ender. Connections need to be made between the book and the child. Bibliotherapy can be conducted with individuals or groups by assigning literature to children for a specific need. If it is used in a small group setting, relationships between participants, book characters and issues, and the facilitator also must be exciting. Open expression should be encouraged. Through the interactive processes of bibliotherapy, emotions are unblocked and emotional pressure relieved. Additionally, by inspection and study of moral values and the spur of critical thinking, the child builds self-awareness, a healthier self-concept, and better social and personal judgment.

Stages

Activities in bibliotherapy should be designed to provide information, provide insight, stimulate discussion, communicate new values and attitudes, create awareness that other people have similar problems, and provide realistic solutions to problems. According to Pardeck (1994), the process goes through four stages:

- Identification
- Selection
- Presentation
- Follow up

The first two stages involve identifying needs and obtaining appropriate books. The creative process takes place during the presentation stage. This is where identification with the character and relevancy of the issue surmises. During the follow up stage, children share what they have gained and pursue the issue. The process can not be inhibited by staying on the surface. Participants must "dig deep."

Benefits

Bibliotherapy has apparent worth in that it offers the chance for people to identify and appreciate themselves, their individuality, and the intricacy of human thought and behavior. It may also promote social development and the love of reading (Gladding & Gladding, 1991). Interest in the use of bibliotherapy appears to have increased in the past few years because of the increase of societal and familial problems in the United States (rise in divorce, alienation of young people, excessive peer pressure, alcohol/drug abuse, and so forth). Educators also have begun to acknowledge the growing need for providing literacy instruction to at-risk and homeless children and their families (Ouzts, 1991). Using books is a simple way to provide for this need. Bibliotherapy is not a end-all cure, but it is an effective technique to use in many situations. When young children are experiencing difficulties in their daily lives, reading about characters with similar problems can help them cope. Experienced therapists use children's books to solve emotional problems. It is not intended to replace counseling or guidance, but only to help ease the concerns and fears of young children in today's world.

How Should it be Used

Arleen Hynes's book, *Bibliotherapy Handbook*, is considered a good all-around introduction to bibliotherapy. It defines the types of bibliotherapy and details what the facilitator needs to know. Bibliotherapy is very versatile. A facilitator can choose whether an individual or group therapy method would be best in the specific setting. According to Pardeck and Pardeck (1990), "groups can be a powerful vehicle for helping to heal emotional problems." The Pardecks believe that a group approach to learning enhances the total child. The group approach allows members to share common experiences, thus lessening anxieties. It can create feelings of belonging and can also provide security for individuals who might feel uncomfortable in situations where they are singled out for special attention. "Working in a group may lead an individual to develop a different perspective and a new understanding of the problems of others" (Bibliotherapy, 1982).

Suggested Criteria for Selection of Literature

Burnett (1997), Huck, Helper, and Hickman (1993), Ouzts (1991), and Rudman (1995) recommended that literature to help children cope with problems have these characteristics:

- Be developmentally appropriate and well written.
- Realistic language in terms of life experiences.
- Depict the honest condition and possibilities for the characters.
- Present multidimensional characters experiencing genuine and relevant emotions.
- Opportunities for debate.
- Explore the working out of problems.
- Show clear communication and responses to children's questions.
- Offer motivational and passionate situations.

Resources for Materials Selection

The following list should be assessable to anyone wanting to use bibliotherapy and literature:

- Cecil, N.L., & Robert, P.L. (1992). *Developing resiliency through children's literature: A guide for teachers and librarians, K-8*. Jefferson, NC: McFarland.

- Dole, P.P. (1990). *Helping children through books: A selected booklist*. Portland, OR: Church and Synagogue Library Association.

- Rasinski, T.V. (1992). *Sensitive issues: An annotated guide to children's literature, K-6*. Phoenix: Oryx Press.

- Rudman, M. (1995). *Children's literature: An issues approach (3rd edition)*. White Plains, NY: Longman.

Conclusion

Through discussions of the problematic issues personified in books, facilitators can help children wrestle with obstacles presented by life itself. Bibliotherapy is a potentially potent system for schools to use on countless levels and in all grades. In order to create a strong program, schools must communicate the process as a non-threatening one. In changing "bibliotherapy" to "biblioguidance," the first step has been taken to create "buy-in." The terms are used indistinguishably. Biblioguidance is the perfect addition to schools that will enhance the total child so that he or she is not only academically strong, but socially and emotionally competent as well.

References

Agnes, S.M. (1946). Bibliotherapy for socially maladjusted children, *Catholic Educational Review*, 44, pp. 8-16.

Bibliotherapy. Fact Sheet (1982). Urbana, IL: ERIC Clearinghouse on Reading and Communication Skills. ED 234 338.

Burnett, J. (1997). *Opening the world to children: Using books to develop problem-solving strategies*. Portland, OR: Annual International Conference of the Association for Childhood Education. [ED414565].

Crothers, S.M. (1916). A literary clinic, *Atlantic Monthly*, 118, pp. 291-301.

Gladding, S.T., & Gladding, C. (1991). The ABCs of bibliotherapy for school counselors. *School Counselor*, 39 (1), 7-13. [EJ 435 466].

Huck, C.S., Henker, S. & Hickman, J. (1993). *Children's literature in the elementary school*. Fort Worth, TX: Harcourt Brace.

Olsen, H.D. (1975). Bibliotherapy to help children solve problems, *Elementary School Journal*, 75, pp. 423-429.

Ouzts, D.T. (1991). The emergence of bibliotherapy as a discipline. *Reading Horizons*, 31 (3), 199-206. [EJ421420].

Pardeck, J.T. (1993). Using literature to help adolescents cope with problems. *Adolescence*, 29 (114), 421-427. [EJ 487 572].

Pardeck, J.T., & Pardeck, J.A. (1989). "Bibliotherapy: A Tool for Helping Preschool Children Deal with Developmental Change Related to Family Relationships." *Early Child Development and Care*, 47, 107-29. EJ 401 179.

Riordan, R.J., & Wilson, L.S. (1989). Bibliotherapy: Does it work? *Journal of Counseling and Development*, 67, pp. 506-507.

Rudman, M. (1995). *Children's literature: An issues approach (3rd edition)*. White Plains, NY: Longman. [Ed379684].

My Program

"Tell me and
I will forget.
Show me and
I will remember.
Involve me and
I will understand."
—Chinese Proverb

In the Beginning

Love of reading… books… children… emotions… counselor… As I was sitting in a class working on my masters in school counseling, a professor asked us the following question, "If you could do anything, create anything, help in anyway with how children learn socially and emotionally, what would you do?" I can remember thinking that I hate it when teachers make us REALLY think instead of just regurgitating information! Since my job was to please the professor, I jotted something down about using books to make a difference with children and closed the journal. That journal wasn't opened again for a couple of years.

Now fast forward about a year. I'm watching the Oprah show (my daily ritual—I think she's a part of my core value system)! It just so happened that I'm watching Oprah on her book club day. I hadn't been reading the book; however, I still watched the show. As the ladies were discussing the book White Oleander an idea struck me—Wouldn't it be a cool idea for the librarian or someone at our school to start a book of the month club to get more children reading and possibly make a difference in their lives? I knew that READERS ARE LEADERS and began to really think about how children + books = success.

Back to the college journal entry… I came across it AFTER writing this book. Amazing! *What's the Issue?* is born! Without even knowing it, somehow ideas came together, I guess subconsciously, and children are being bettered! I trust that everything happens for a reason even if I can't always figure it out. The information that follows is what I've been doing. I encourage everyone to tailor a program that works for you and your school. I share the details of how I work my program so that ideas may be gained to "get your wheels turning". I love what Oprah says about growth "The whole point of being alive is to evolve into the complete person you were intended to be." Whether we are talking people or programs, keep working, tweaking, and growing until you reach completion. Completion usually means success!

Before beginning a biblioguidance program, the most time-consuming endeavor is creating an effective book list of children's literature, based on life issues topics such as worry, fear, anger, and so forth. There are SO MANY children's books available! Some good—some not so good. I find it amazing that some characters and situations practically "leap" off the page into the lives of children to give them hope and a unique learning opportunity. It is also important to establish a relationship with local libraries and bookstores. Keeping them updated on the club and issues makes it easy for families to obtain the books and stay "plugged in."

Once school starts, I send home a guidance and counseling needs assessment so I can get an idea of common issues children are having in our district. A bilingual copy of my assessment is in the appendix of this book. When I get that information back, I start to set topics for each session I will conduct. My biblioguidance program is in the form of a monthly book club called *"What's the Issue?"* I display book club information on bulletin boards, websites, newsletters, and the newspaper. I send home bilingual sign up sheets and information about the program once in September and again in January. These go home to everyone. Parents must sign children up, either for first semester, second semester, or by topic.

By having two sign ups, there is more availability of spaces. If there are certain children who have been referred to me for the topic that will be covered, I may also contact the parent by phone to discuss the child participating. I have cutoff numbers at 20 per grade level; that is a workable-sized group. Parents also must put first and second choices for topics. If more children sign up than 20 for a particular session, I take the children whose forms I received back first into the sessions first. Sometimes, I may create another time for a club to meet to accommodate more children. After setting up the groups, I send home letters informing all families who signed up as to the situation (whether they got in the group and which one). For children who don't get into the club, I find alternative ways to offer help (individual, group counseling, or some other type of guidance). I give all students who signed up copies of discussion questions and activities, even if they aren't going to meet with the club. This has not been a problem so far!

The Sessions

Once the book club numbers and children are in place, I begin designing the session. I hold my meetings in October, November, January, February, and May. Since August, December, and March are short months because of holiday breaks, book club doesn't meet. We also don't meet in April because everyone is usually involved in testing. Times and days are flexible. I have had the club during lunch, with the children eating in my room. However, currently I have club after school one week out of the month. Mondays start with kindergarten, Tuesday is first grade, Wednesday is second grade, Thursday is third grade, and Friday is fourth grade. It is very important to stress attendance and the pickup time of children to parents because some other children may not get to come because the group is full. If things come up, have the parents notify you so you can try and add someone to the group.

My first session in October starts with a "bang." I use "worry" as the first session because children commonly feel this at the beginning of the year. I also have more activities and "hoopla" planned around the first session. This gets everyone excited and interested in what is going on in book club. In the first section (worry) of this book, you will find everything you need to conduct this session.

First, I put up the display information. After doing that, I send home the party invitation, discussion sheet (one week before meeting), and headband activity encouraging children to get excited about our first meeting. The children are also told to wear the Mouse Ears Headband (more advertising) on the day of book club and come prepared to discuss and have fun! Basically, after that I just prepare the topic and wait until the day of the meeting. On the day of the first meeting, I make the food and drink recipes that go along with the book and set out coloring pages and so forth for children to start. Once everyone arrives, we get started by following the agenda. There is always discussion time of the book, issues, and personal relevancy, as well as an interactive activity. I end all book clubs by sending a parent letter home and having a drawing for a club T-shirt.

All sessions aren't as elaborate as the first, but I do try to start and end in a way that really promotes the club. The more children I proactively introduce to these topics, the fewer "fires" I have to put out later. In the past I have ended with the friendship session, which is also included in this book. I do a pizza party for the children, and we wrap up all issues and fill out evaluations.

Misc. Information

Each family is responsible for either checking out the book at a library or purchasing it at a local bookstore. ONE OF EVERY BOOK WITHIN EACH TOPIC IS A BILINGUAL CHILDREN'S BOOK AVAILABLE IN VARIOUS LANGUAGES. This helps with parents at home being involved in the process of growing with the child socially and emotionally. Usually in the information that goes home to parents, I make a few suggestions as to where the book can be located. Grants (use the research already provided) or local scholarships are another alternative to gaining more books for your program. The children's responsibilities are to read the book and review the discussion page BEFORE coming to book club.

I am continually designing, changing, and working to make this program more valuable. In the future, I am hoping to do this district-wide (appropriate level books) with some sort of summer camp-type experience. In Prosper ISD, we also have a foundation set up that awards grants to different programs. In applying for the grant, I received money to buy copies of books to use with the underprivileged children we serve. Another great resource for Title I schools is First Books. You can locate them at www.firstbook.org. At the end of year, I also send home evaluation forms to students and parents, asking them for feedback. These evaluations are included in the appendix.

If you are interested in receiving a CD or disk of discussion pages and parent letters for use with the computer, or other additional supplies or materials associated with this book, please call (972) 347-2236.

Worry

"Some books leave us free and some books make us free."

—Ralph Waldo Emerson

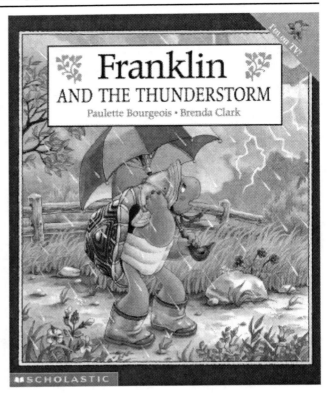

Choose a book—

Wemberly Worried
or
Franklin and the Thunderstorm

Make a poster to promote the book club.

Worry Agenda

I. Read the chosen book together. (5 minutes)

II. Group Discussion questions. (10 minutes)

III. So Don't Worry exercise... (5 minutes)

IV. Worry Wart Lesson. (15 minutes)

Send home parent letter

Remind about next book club

Draw for shirt

If using Wemberly Worried

Prior to the first book club, I send out the invitation to participants (to get them excited) as well as the mouse ears instructions. I encourage them to make the mouse ears and wear them to school on their book club day. This really gets students talking about book club and is a good "advertisement." I also make some of the recipes to nibble on during book club. I have *Wemberly's Search,* (p. 36), *The Coloring Page*, (p. 37), and *Mouse Maze*, (p. 38), in the room when they come in to get them started until everyone gets there. DON'T WORRY, I don't go to all this trouble every time; but, I want to make the first time special and comfortable. It also gets everyone excited!

Preoccupation

Prudencia Se Preocupa

Kevin Henkes

LOS OBJETIVOS:

- ✓ Los participantes serán capaces de definir qué preocupación es.
- ✓ Los participantes serán capaces de demostrar una comprensión que si las circunstancias que ellos se preocupan por implica sus pensamientos, los sentimientos, las elecciones, y la conducta entonces ellos tienen el control del sujeto.
- ✓ Los participantes serán capaces de identificar eso hay algunas circunstancias que ellos no pueden controlar.
- ✓ Los participantes serán capaces de identificar qué preocupaciones comunes son para su nivel de desarrollo.

Las preguntas para la Discusión del Grupo

(Está listo para discutir estas preguntas con todo detalle y la acción experimenta relacionado a ellos.)

1. ¿Qué preocupa significa?
2. ¿Qué era algunos de las preocupaciones que Wemberly tuvo en el cuento?
3. ¿Qué es algunos de sus preocupaciones?
   ¿Tuvo Wemberly parte de las mismas preocupaciones como usted?
4. ¿En el libro, las personas dijeron Wemberly para no preocupar. personas.
   Do jamás lo dicen que y cómo lo hace se siente?
5. ¿Se preocupó Wemberly por el campo de juegos al colegio...
   Do que usted se preocupa jamás por eso?
   ¿Qué preocupa usted acerca de en el campo de juegos?
6. ¿Qué lo hace se siente mejor cuando usted está preocupado?
7. Wemberly no estaba preocupado por "quedando en" al colegio.
   ¿Se preocupa jamás usted por eso?
   ¿Qué no es la cosa buena y mala acerca de "quedando en?"

Available in Spanish

Worry and Anxiety

Wemberly Worried

Kevin Henkes

OBJECTIVES:

✓ Participants will be able to define what worry is.

✓ Participants will be able to demonstrate an understanding that if the circumstances they worry about involves their thoughts, feelings, choices, and behavior then they have control of the subject.

✓ Participants will be able to identify that there are some circumstances that they cannot control.

✓ Participants will be able to identify what common worries are for their developmental level.

Questions for Group Discussion

(Be ready to discuss these questions in detail and share experiences related to them.)

1. What does worry mean?

2. What were some of the worries that Wemberly had in the story?

3. What are some of your worries?
   Did Wemberly have some of the same worries as you?

4. In the book, people told Wemberly not to worry...
   Do people ever tell you that and how does that make you feel?

5. Wemberly worried about the playground at school...
   Do you ever worry about that?
   What do you worry about on the playground?

6. What makes you feel better when you are worried?

7. Wemberly was worried about not "fitting in" at school.
   Do you ever worry about that?
   What is the good thing about not "fitting in" and what is the bad thing about not "fitting in?"

Preocupación

Franklin En La Oscuridad

Paulette Bourgeois

OBJETIVOS:

- ✓ Los participantes discutirán preocupaciones que aquejan a los niños.
- ✓ Los participants identificarán como las preocupaciones afectan a la gente.
- ✓ Los participantes discutirán la presión de los compañeros.
- ✓ Los participantes discutirán la perspectiva y como se relaciona a la preocupación.
- ✓ Los participantes planearán maneras para sobreponerse a la preocupación.

Las preguntas para la Discusión del Grupo

(Está listo para discutir estas preguntas con todo detalle y la acción experimenta relacionado a ellos.)

1. La mayor preocupación de Franklin eran las tormentas. ¿Qué tipo de cosas te preocupan?

2. Franklin no iba a ir a la casa de sus amigos porque estaba preocupado por la tormenta, pero su mamá lo animó a ir. ¿Te ayuda cuando la gente te anima a sobreponerte a tus preocupaciones? ¿Por qué o por qué no?

3. Franklin se sintió inquieto por dentro al ver que la tormenta se acerc aba. ¿Qué tipo de señales te da tu cuerpo cuando estas preocupado o temeroso?

4. A todos los amigos de Franklin no les preocupaban las tormentas. ¿Qué hace que alguna gente se preocupe por cosas y otras no? ¿Crees que experiencias que tiene la gente influencían sus preocupaciones?

5. ¿Qué es la presión de los compañeros? En el cuento, los amigos de Franklin lo convencen de ir a la casa del árbol para guarecerse. ¿Fue ese un buen plan? ¿Por qué o por qué no? ¿Tienen siempre los amigos todas las respuestas correctas para nuestros temores y preocupaciones?

6. ¿Te hacen querer esconderte el miedo y la preocupación? ¿Crees que sea una buena o mala idea? ¿Qué pasa si dejas que la preocupación o el miedo te controlen así?

7. Los amigos de Franklin vieron a las tormentas de un modo diferente teniendo pensamientos chistosos acerca de lo que estaría pasando en las nubes. ¿Qué es perspectiva? ¿Crees que el modo en que ves las cosas influencía tus preocupaciones?

8. La tormenta que preocupó a Franklin pasó y todo salió bien. Dime acerca de algo que en alguna ocasión realmente te preocupó pero todo salió bien. ¿Te preocupaste por nada? ¿Preocuparte cambió algo? ¿Cuáles son algunas cosas que puedes hacer cuando estás realmente preocupado para ayudarte a sobreponerte a esos sentimientos?

9. ¿Cómo puedes comparar una tormenta con nuestras vidas?

Available in Spanish

Worry and Anxiety

Franklin and the Thunderstorm
Paulette Bourgeois

OBJECTIVES:

- ✓ Participants will discuss different worries of children.
- ✓ Participants will identify how worry affects people.
- ✓ Participants will discuss peer pressure.
- ✓ Participants will discuss perspective and how it relates to worry.
- ✓ Participants will strategize ways to overcome worry.

Questions for Group Discussion

(Be ready to discuss these questions in detail and share experiences related to them.)

1. Franklin's big worry was storms. What kinds of things do you worry about?

2. Franklin was going to not go to his friends house because he was worried about the storm, but his mother encouraged him to go on. Does it help when people encourage you to overcome your worries? Why or why not?

3. Franklin felt jumpy inside as he saw the storm approaching. What kind of signs does your body give you when you are worried or fearful?

4. All of Franklin's friends were not worried about thunderstorms. What makes some people worry about things and others not? Do you think people's experiences influence their worries?

5. What is peer pressure? In the story Franklin's friends talked him into going to the treehouse for shelter. Was that a good plan? Why or why not? Do friends always have the right answers to our fears and worries?

6. Does fear or worry make you want to "crawl into your shell?" Do you think that is a good idea or bad idea? What happens if you let worry or fear control you like that?

7. Franklin's friends looked at storms in a different way by thinking funny thoughts about what was going on in the clouds. What is perspective? Do you think that the way you look at things influences what you worry about?

8. The storm Franklin worried about passed and everything worked out okay. Tell me about a time when you really worried about something and it worked out okay. Did you worry for nothing? Does worry change anything? What are some things you can do when you are really worried to help you overcome your feelings?

9. How can you compare a storm to our lives?

We're Having a Party!

Date: _____

Time: _____

Place: _____

*Be there for books,
activities and fun.*

Lots of mice needed!

Mouse Ears Headband

Materials needed:

- Construction paper
- Pencil
- Glue
- Large cup
- Small cup

What to Do:

Step One: Cut out a black strip of construction paper to wrap around your child's forehead. Make it about two inches wide and leave an extra inch lengthwise for the last step.

Step Two: Fold a black piece of construction paper in half. Trace two circles from the cup onto the paper and cut them out.

Step Three: Trace two circles with the smaller cup onto pink construction paper.

Step Four: Cut out the pink circles and glue one in the middle of each black circle. These are the ears.

Step Five: Put an edge of each ear up against the strip of paper and glue them in place.

Step Six: When the glue dries, staple or tape the ends of the strip together to fit snugly round your child's forehead.

Wemberly's Search

```
G  Z  V  R  V  S  S  R  M  I  Y  D  I  H  X
Y  X  U  Z  H  M  D  J  E  W  E  L  K  O  R
F  V  L  N  H  A  C  N  J  S  B  D  Z  S  L
S  J  Z  B  B  P  O  S  E  J  G  L  Y  E  D
Q  H  L  Q  C  C  V  O  V  I  Z  E  A  D  Q
I  G  E  F  Z  Q  I  F  V  T  R  R  B  R  S
X  L  M  O  F  I  R  Y  S  S  N  F  I  U  O
Y  Y  J  Q  F  S  Q  Q  T  I  L  K  Z  M  M
F  M  N  N  K  G  X  Y  N  G  J  I  P  S  L
M  U  H  C  A  E  P  G  T  N  A  N  D  N  J
Y  S  O  E  L  X  R  G  T  I  L  U  B  E  C
D  L  X  N  L  J  V  D  S  R  P  G  T  P  H
B  Z  W  Q  T  E  T  W  T  A  N  O  X  C  G
M  A  B  X  G  Q  U  Z  N  H  Y  O  Y  A  X
E  B  G  C  N  U  X  M  F  S  B  C  H  Z  T
```

(Mrs. Peachum, Jewel, Friends, Slide, Blocks, Drums, Sharing, Toys, Learning)

The Coloring Page

(Everyone can be an artist!)

Mouse Maze

DeDe Coffman

So Don't Worry

Objective: To illustrate how worrying works by taking away your happiness.

Materials: Copies of the picture handout, page 40

Procedure: First give each child a copy of the handout, and have them look over the pictures. Explain to the class that everything on the page is something enjoyable. Having a happy birthday, getting a shiny new bike, being able to play in "the big game of the season", going to the circus, and of course, getting a new little puppy. Ask the children what they like best. Begin explaining that worrying can take away from being able to fully enjoy these things. Ask them what types of things they worry about.

Example:

Worrying about getting a good grade on a test.

Worrying about whether other children will like you.

Worrying about your mom or dad finding out you did something wrong.

Worrying about what others will think if you don't do well at sports.

Worrying about the way you look.

As you share examples of worrying, have children tear off one picture if they have ever worried about the same thing. Give other examples and have them continue to tear off pictures when they agree with the statement. Pretty soon the children will have little or nothing left.

Explain that this is how worrying works. If we spend too much time worrying, or if we worry about too many things, what should be fun and happy isn't any more. So what should we do... (now begin next activity-Worry Warts)

Happy Birthday!

Playing the big game!

Shiny, new bike!

New little puppy!

A day at the circus!

Worry Wart Lesson

Objective:

1. The student will be able to define worry.

2. The student will be able to demonstrate an understanding that if the circumstances they worry about involves their thoughts, feelings, choices, and behavior they have control of the subject.

3. The student will be able to identify that there are some circumstances that they cannot control.

4. Encourage students to learn healthy responses to worry.

Materials: Index card with worry poem already on it, rocks, eyes, cotton filler, glue, markers.

Procedure: Ask the class for a definition of worry. Point out that people do not often worry about good things (for example: winning the lottery). Emphasize that just because something bad might happen, DOESN'T mean it will happen!

Compare Wemberly's worries to the worries in the Don't worry lesson.

Discuss two things to do with worry: let the worry go or do something!

Activity: Students will make worry warts so they can give their worries away.

1. Give students the index card of "Worry, Worry, Worry." (Help them learn this.)

2. Place glue on the index card and attach the rock.

3. Glue eyes on rock.

4. Glue cotton to the rock for hair.

5. Color the hair with marker.

POEM

Worry, Worry, Worry

It makes your thinking blurry!

When you can't change a worry of any sort

Just give the worry to the worry wart!

Worry Questionnaire

Directions: This form is about worrying. Worrying happens when you are scared about something and you think about it a lot. People sometimes worry about school, families, health, future, and so forth. Read each sentence and circle the answer that best tells how true that sentence is about you.

1. My worries really bother me. Never true sometimes true always true

2. I don't really worry about things. Never true sometimes true always true

3. Many things make me worry. Never true sometimes true always true

4. I just can't help worrying. Never true sometimes true always true

5. When I'm under pressure, I worry a lot. Never true sometimes true always true

6. I find it easy to stop worrying. Never true sometimes true always true

7. I've been a worrier all my life. Never true sometimes true always true

8. I worry about things until they are done. Never true sometimes true always true

9. When I finish one thing, I start to worry about everything else. Never true sometimes true always true

Date

Dear Parents,

Our first session of *"What's the Issue?"* went well. The children were really enthusiastic and involved in our discussions and activities. They should have a much better understanding of what worry is and the destructive things that worry can do to us. I encourage you to visit with your child about our session and further reinforce the social-emotional learning that took place. You know sometimes we forget that everyone has problems whether they may come from work, school, or anywhere else. It's how we look at those problems that makes all the difference in the world. I believe that children need to know from an early age that life has ups and downs and that we do not live in a perfect society... And most important, that WE HAVE CHOICES on how we react to our problems.

Children need to know healthy ways to communicate and react. Worry is a very normal part of life for all of us; however, if you believe your child worries so much that it affects their behavior or personality, please feel free to call me. On the back of this form is some questions that may help you determine types of worry and the degree to which worry may be interfering with a child's everyday life. A really great book for parents dealing with children's worries is *Seven Steps to Help Your Child Worry Less* by Sam Goldstein, Ph.D. This is a great book that helps you with strategies and developing plans to help your child manage worry, fear, and anxiety. Two simple steps to take if you child is one who worries a lot are 1) Identify what your child is worried about by talking over his concerns and 2) Work with your child to come up with ways of dealing with the worry such as role-playing or obtaining more information about the worrisome situation.

I hope that your child comes home today enlightened and ready to take on his/her worries completely. Let me know if I can be of further help. A great place to get most of the books is on Amazon.com, and it is usually the cheapest as well. Don't forget next month's "What's the Issue?" session is during the week of November 17-21 on anger with *When Sophie Gets Angry* by Molly Bang. You may always pick up your children in front of the elementary after our sessions. I will walk them out. PLEASE MAKE SURE TO INCLUDE A NOTE IN YOUR CHILD'S FOLDER ON THE DAY OF BOOK CLUB SO THAT HE/SHE KNOWS TO LEAVE THEM WITH ME!!!

Sincerely,

Name

Title

La Fecha

Estimados Padres,

Nuestra primera sesión de *"lo que Es el Asunto"* fue bien. Los niños estaban realmente entusiasmados e implicados en nuestra discusión y actividades. Ellos deben tener una comprensión mucho más mejor de lo que preocupa es y las cosas destructivas que preocupan pueden hacer a nosotros. Yo lo aliento a visitar con su niño acerca de nuestra sesión y reforzar aún más el aprender social-emocional que sucedió. Usted sabe a veces que nosotros nos olvidamos que todos tienen los problemas si ellos pueden venir del trabajo, la escuela, o dondequiera más. Es cómo miramos esos problemas que hace toda la diferencia en el mundo. Creo que niños necesitan saber de una edad temprana que esa vida tiene arriba y hacia abajo y que nosotros no vivimos en una sociedad perfecta... And muy importante, que TENEMOS las ELECCIONES en cómo reaccionamos a nuestros problemas.

Los niños necesitan saber las maneras sanas comunicar y reaccionar. La preocupación es una parte muy normal de la vida para todos nosotros; sin embargo, si usted cree que su niño preocupa tanto que afecta su conducta o la personalidad, se sienten por favor libre llamarme. En la espalda de esta forma es algunos preguntan eso lo puede ayudar a determinar los tipos de la preocupación y el grado a que preocupan puede estar interviniendo con una vida cotidiana de niño. Un libro realmente gran para padres que tratan con preocupaciones de niños es Siete Pasos de Ayudar Su Preocupación de Niño Menos por Sam Goldstein, Ph.D. Esto es un gran libro que ayuda usted con estrategias y planes reveladores ayudar a su niño maneja la preocupación, el temor, y la ansiedad. Dos pasos sencillos de tomar si su niño es uno que preocupa alot es 1) Identifica lo que su niño está preocupado por discute su concierne y 2) el Trabajo con su niño para proponer las maneras de tratar con la preocupación tal como papel-jugando u obteniendo más información acerca de la situación inquietante.

Espero que su niño venga en casa hoy culto y se prepara para tomar sus preocupaciones completamente. Permita que mí sepa si puedo ser de ayuda adicional. Un gran lugar para obtener la mayor parte de los libros están en el Amazonas.com, y son generalmente el más barato también. No olvídese luego mes "lo que el Asunto" la sesión está durante la semana de noviembre 17-21 en la cólera con When Sophie Gets Angry por Molly Bang. Usted siempre puede recoger a sus niños delante del elemental después de nuestras sesiones. Yo los andaré fuera. ¡CERCIOREse POR FAVOR para INCLUIR UNA NOTA EN SU CARPETA de NIÑO EN EL DIA DE el CLUB del LIBRO PARA QUE EL/ELLA SEPA SALIRLOS CONMIGO!!

Sinceramente,

Nombre
Titulo

What Do Kids Worry About?

By Dr. Linda S. Mintle, Ph.D

Stress has increased for kids over recent decades. Life is lived faster. Social structures like the family are breaking down leaving kids more vulnerable to stress and anxiety. The result is more kids suffer from stress related illnesses. Childhood emotional disorders are more prevalent than ever before and pediatricians see record number of kids for physically related stress illness.

Do you wonder what children worry about?

Researchers Silverman, LaGreca, and Wasserstein (1995) decided to study the normal worries of schoolchildren between the ages of 7 and 12 years. They interviewed 273 schoolchildren and asked them about 14 areas of worry. When a child identified a specific area of worry, the researchers asked more detailed questions. Here's what they found.

✓ The average number of worries per child was 7.64 and covered a wide range of topics but most worried about health, school, and personal harm.

✓ The most frequent worries were about family, classmates, and friends.

✓ The most intense worries were about war, money, and disasters.

✓ Children's worries related somewhat to anxiety.

Another community study (Henker, Whalen, & O'Neil, 1995) interviewed 194 children in grades four through eight to find out their worries and risk perceptions about health and the environment. These kids identified concerns about personal issues (e.g., grades), social relations, death, and social issues such as homelessness and the environment.

When you ask kids what they would like to change the most in their lives, the answer is frequently to have parents who are less stressed and tired. Children are reacting to what researchers Miller and Rahe have documented—stress has increased 45% over the past 30 years.

Information about normal childhood worries also helps us understand the role of worry in children developing anxiety disorders. Weems, Silverman, and La Greca (2000) took the normative data on childhood worries and compared it to anxious children referred to specialty clinics. When they did, they found that clinic kids worried about similar concerns. However, anxious kids tend to worry more often, more intensely, and more of the time.

As parents, we need to seriously think of ways to decrease the stress in our homes. Kids need down time and an opportunity to practice relaxation. If you find yourselves running from event to event, it's time to slow down and rethink priorities. Both you and your children will benefit from the changes.

Questions for Worry Assessment—www.samgoldstein.com "Paying Attention to the Inflation of Worry"

Does your child persistently talk about, or seem preoccupied with a particular stress or fear?

Has the child's sleeping habits changed? (nightmares, avoidance of going to sleep, waking during night)

Does the child avoid activities or situation that were previously enjoyed?

Does the child complain of physical symptoms, particularly before certain activities like school?

Does the child cry or appear easily bothered by minor things?

Does the child appear jumpy, tense, or on "pins and needles?"

Does the child avoid sleepovers?

Has the child's schoolwork or enthusiasm declined?

Has the child reduced time with friends?

Has the child's appetite changed?

Qué Hace los Niños se Preocupan Por

By Dr. Linda S. Mintle, Ph.D

El énfasis ha aumentado para niños sobre décadas recientes. La vida se vive más rápida. Las estructuras sociales quieren que la familia sea la partida rota los niños más vulnerables de enfatizar y la ansiedad. El resultado es más niños sufren del énfasis las enfermedades relacionadas. La niñez los desórdenes emocionales son más predominantes que jamás antes y los pediatras ven el número sin precedentes de niños para la enfermedad físicamente relacionada del énfasis.

¿Se pregunta usted a qué niños se preocupan por? Los investigadores Silverman, LaGreca, y Wasserstein (1995) decidieron estudiar las preocupaciones normales de alumno entre las edades de 7 y 12 años. Ellos entrevistaron a 273 alumno y los preguntó acerca de 14 áreas de la preocupación. Cuándo un niño identificó un área específica de la preocupación, los investigadores preguntaron más detalló las preguntas. Aquí está lo que ellos encontraron.

- ✓ El número medio de preocupaciones por niño era 7.64 y cubrió una gran variedad de temas pero de la mayoría del se preocupó por la salud, por la escuela, y por el daño personal.

- ✓ El preocupa normalmente estaban acerca de la familia, acerca de los compañeros de clase, y acerca de los amigos.

- ✓ Las preocupaciones más intensas estaban acerca de la guerra, acerca del dinero, y acerca de los desastres.

- ✓ Las preocupaciones de niños relacionaron algo a la ansiedad.

Otro estudio de la comunidad (Henker, cazar ballenas, & O'Neil, 1995) entrevistó a 194 niños en grados cuatro por ocho en averiguar sus percepciones de preocupaciones y riesgo acerca de la salud y el ambiente. Estos niños identificados conciernen acerca de asuntos personales (por ejemplo, los grados), las relaciones sociales, la muerte, y los asuntos sociales tales como la falta de vivienda y el ambiente

Cuándo usted pregunta los niños lo que ellos querrían cambiar el la mayoría del en su vive, la respuesta deberá tener con frecuencia a padres que son enfatizados menos y se es cansado. Los niños reaccionan a qué Molinero de investigadores y Rahe ha documentado — stress ha aumentado 45% sobre los pasados 30 años. Cuando padres, nosotros necesitamos pensar gravemente en maneras de disminuir el énfasis en nuestros hogares. La necesidad de niños hacia abajo tiempo y una oportunidad de practicar la relajación. Si usted se encuentran huyendo el acontecimiento al acontecimiento, es tiempo de ir más despacio y volver a pensar las prioridades. Ambos usted y sus niños beneficiarán de los cambios.

Las preguntas para la Evaluación —www.samgoldstein.com

¿Hace a su niño persistentemente discurso acerca de, o parece preocupado con cierto énfasis o el temor?

¿Tiene al niño es los hábitos durmientes cambiados?

¿Evita el niño las actividades o las situaciones que se gozaron previamente?

¿Llora el niño o aparece fácilmente molestado por cosas secundarias?

¿Aparece el niño nervioso, tenso, o en "hormigueos?"

¿Evita el niño sleepovers?

¿Han disminuido el trabajo escolar del niño o el entusiasmo?

¿Ha reducido el niño tiempo con amigos?

¿Ha cambiado el apetito del niño?

Anger

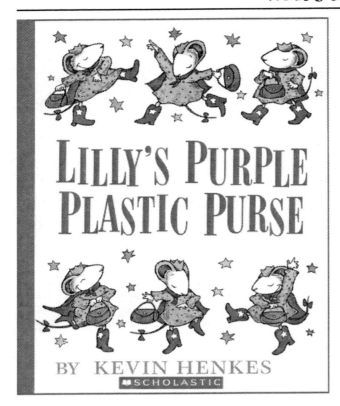

Choose a book—

Lilly's Purple Plastic Purse
or
When Sophie Gets Angry Really,
Really, Really Angry

Make a poster to promote the book club.

Anger Agenda

I. Read one of the stories together. (5 minutes)

II. Group Discussion questions. (10 minutes)

III. Go over anger worksheet. (body signs, effects, what to do). (5 minutes)

IV. Have them answer "How Does Your Body Talk?" (5 minutes)

V. Anger illustrations through science experiment. (Bo Bottlehead). (15 minutes)

Send home parent letter

Remind about next book club

Draw for shirt

la Cólera

Lily y su Bolso de Plastico Morado

Kevin Henkes

LOS OBJETIVOS:

✓ Los participantes serán capaces de definir qué cólera es.

✓ Los participantes serán capaces de demostrar una comprensión que enoja está bien, pero que's cómo usted trata con lo que importa.

✓ Los participantes serán capaces de identificar las maneras positivas para expresar la cólera.

✓ Los participantes serán capaces de identificar qué circunstancias comunes hacen los niños enojados.

Las preguntas para la Discusión del Grupo

(Está listo para discutir estas preguntas con todo detalle y la acción experimenta relacionado a ellos.)

1. ¿Qué significa estar enojado?

2. ¿De que estaba Lilly enojada en este cuento? ¿Cómo supiste? ¿Que debería haber hecho Lilly en el cuento?

3. ¿Cómo trató Lilly al Sr. Slinger cuando estaba enojada? ¿Cómo tratas a la gente cuando estás enojado? ¿Cómo trató Lilly a sus compañeros de clase? ¿Fue respetuosa?

4. En el libro, ¿Trató Lilly de eliminar su enoja de una manera positiva o negativa? ¿Funcionó? ¿Cómo habría manejado su enojo en una manera positiva?

5. ¿Te has sentido mal alguna vez por la manera en que manejaste tu enojo? ¿Qué hizo Lilly para contentarse con el Sr. Slinger? ¿Qué puedes hacer para contenarte con alguien después de haberte enojado?

6. ¿Qué hace tu cuerpo cuando te empiezas a enojar?

7. ¿Qué es paciencia? ¿Está la paciencia conectada al enojo? ¿Ha intervenido la ira con tu vida, sueños, o metas? ¿Cómo?

Available in Spanish

Lilly's Purple Plastic Purse

Kevin Henkes

OBJECTIVES:

- ✓ Participants will be able to define what anger is.
- ✓ Participants will be able to demonstrate an understanding that anger is okay, but that it's how you deal with it that matters.
- ✓ Participants will be able to identify positive ways to express anger.
- ✓ Participants will be able to identify what common circumstances make kids angry.

Questions for Group Discussion

(Be ready to discuss these questions in detail and share experiences related to them.)

1. What does being angry mean?
2. What was Lilly angry about in the story? How did you know? What should Lilly have been with in the story?
3. How did Lilly treat Mr. Slinger when she was angry? How do you treat people when you are angry? How did Lilly treat her classmates? Was she respectful?
4. In the book, did Lilly try to get rid of her anger in a positive or negative way? Did it work? How might she have vented her anger in a positive way?
5. Have you ever felt bad about how you handled your anger? What did Lilly do to make things right with Mr. Slinger? What can after taking your anger out on someone to make things right?
6. What does your body do when you begin to get angry?
7. What is patience? Is patience connected to anger? Does anger ever interfere with your life, dreams, or goals? How?

la Cólera

Cuando Sofia Se Enoja, Se Enoja de Veras

Molly Bang

OBJETIVOS:

- ✓ Los participantes podrán definir lo que es la ira.
- ✓ Los participantes podrán demostrar un entendimiento de que está bien enojarse, pero que lo importante es como manejes ese enojo.
- ✓ Los participantes podrán identificar maneras positivas para expresar enojo.
- ✓ Los participantes podrán identificar circunstancias comunes que hacen a los niños enojarse.

Las preguntas para la Discusión del Grupo

(Está listo para discutir estas preguntas con todo detalle y la acción experimenta relacionado a ellos.)

1. ¿Qué es ira? ¿Es buena o mala?
2. ¿Cómo te hacen enojar otras personas? ¿Cómo deberías manejar ese enojo?
3. ¿Cuáles fueron algunas maneras en que Sophie manejo su enojo? ¿Has pateado, gritado, o golpeado alguna vez?
4. ¿De que manera son similares el enojo y un volcán?
5. ¿Es correr una buena manera de manejar tu enojo? ¿De que otra manera puedes liberarte de tu enojo?
6. ¿Puedes ver la belleza del mundo cuando estás enojado?

Available in Spanish

When Sophie Get Angry
Really, Really, Really Angry

Molly Bang

OBJECTIVES:

- ✓ Participants will be able to define what anger is.
- ✓ Participants will be able to demonstrate an understanding that anger is okay, but that it's how you deal with it that matters.
- ✓ Participants will be able to identify positive ways to express anger.
- ✓ Participants will be able to identify what common circumstances make kids angry.

Questions for Group Discussion

(Be ready to discuss these questions in detail and share experiences related to them.)

1. What is anger? Is it bad or good?

2. How do other people make you angry? How should you handle this anger?

3. What were some of the ways Sophie vented her anger? Have you ever kicked, screamed, or smashed?

4. How is anger and a volcano similar?

5. Is running a good way to release your anger? What are some other ways you can let go of your anger?

6. Can you see the world's beauty when you're angry?

Anger

Body signs of Anger

1. feeling tense or shaky
2. clutched fists or teeth
3. rising blood pressure (red face or neck)
4. increased heart rate
5. raised voice or yelling
6. wanting to kick, hit or throw
7. adrenaline rush
8. breathing faster
9. mean thoughts

Effects on Anger on our Health

1. headaches
2. breathing problems
3. skin disorders
4. nervous system problem
5. emotional problems
6. suicide

I'm angry now what...

1. Stop and take a deep breath... count to five.
2. Focus on your breathing in and out.
3. Count from ten to one backward slowly; keep counting until calm.
4. Consider your options. Think about what might happen.
5. Decide what to do, but keep your hands to yourself.
6. Tell the person how you feel using an "I" message.
7. Listen and try to work out a solution with respect.
8. Talk about the problem to a trusted friend.
9. Think happy thoughts... you've done all you can do.

Things you can do when Angry...

1. Write out your angry feelings in a journal or letter.
2. Draw a picture of your anger.
3. Do exercises or running.
4. Crumple up a piece of paper.
5. Smash a pillow or clay.
6. Sing.
7. Remember that getting back at someone never makes it better.
8. Remember **GET YOUR ANGER OUT RESPECTFULLY!**

How Does Your Body Talk?
(your anger signs)

1. When your anger has been aroused/ triggered what are the PHYSICAL signs?

❏ Furrowed brow   ❏ Clenched fists   ❏ Headache

❏ Fixed jaw   ❏ Knots in stomach   ❏ Feeling light-headed, confused

❏ Lump in throat   Tightness in intestines   ❏ Rapid heartbeat

❏ Clenched teeth   ❏ Tense muscles   ❏ Heavy breathing, sweating

❏ Tight neck   ❏ Backache   ❏ Insomnia

❏ Tense shoulders   ❏ Other physical signs (describe)

2. When your anger has been aroused/triggered what are the FEELINGS signs?

❏ Tense   ❏ Abandoned   ❏ Frustrated

❏ Insecure   ❏ Left out   ❏ Embarrassed

❏ Misunderstood   ❏ Hostile   ❏ Humiliated

❏ Criticized/judged   ❏ Threatened   ❏ Fearful

❏ Hurt   ❏ Cornered   ❏ Irritable

3. When your anger has been aroused/triggered what are the BEHAVIORAL signs?

❏ Increased desire for drugs (including nicotine)   ❏ Aggressive tone of voice

❏ Increased alcohol intake   ❏ Closed-minded   ❏ Avoid others

❏ Silence   ❏ Foot tapping   ❏ Argumentative

❏ Voice getting louder   ❏ Abrupt gestures   ❏ Pouting

❏ Revenge fantasies   ❏ Close to tears   ❏ Silent treatment

❏ Being snappy

4. Ways my body is telling me that my anger has been aroused:

Angry Explosion

Objectives: The students will recognize how ignoring the signs of anger and internalizing angry feelings can lead to a buildup of anger that might cause problems for them. They will also describe ways to express and manage anger.

Materials: (per small group) Baking soda, vinegar, small narrow mouthed bottle (like a coke bottle), cork or rubber stopper to fit the end of the bottle (alternative- balloon to fit over the neck of the bottle).

Procedure:

1. Set up by having the baking soda in a dish and the narrow mouthed bottle, stopper, and a small container of vinegar nearby. Ask the students to brainstorm with you about "Bo the Bottlehead's" day. Have them come up with things that might have irritated Bo or caused him to feel angry. Each time they come up with an idea, put a pinch of baking soda in the bottle. Question: "Is Bo letting any of these feelings out?"

2. After brainstorming, say to the students, "When you keep angry feelings inside with- out doing anything about them, eventually your body has a reaction to them. You produce chemicals called hormones, which cause your body to react to these feelings. What are some of the things you feel in your body when you get angry?

3. Say, "Bo has held his anger in all day. Finally, something happens and he can't keep it in any longer. It might be a little thing, or it might be a big thing. Pour the vinegar into the bottle, then quickly place the stopper in the bottle (or balloon over the neck). This is a good time to discuss things they have done when they are angry that are inappropriate. (If the explosion doesn't work the first time, use it as more ammunition for making Bo madder).

4. After the "explosion", ask the students, "What could Bo have done to help him get rid of all those bad feelings so he didn't feel like he had to explode? List all coping mecha- nisms on board!

Date

Dear Parents,

"What's the Issue?" was very exciting today. The children were very open and learned much about the often, misunderstood emotion of anger. According to research from www.athealth.com anger has three components. First, the child has what's called the emotional state of anger, which is where the child begins to feel the frustration of a goal being blocked or needs going unmet. Second, the child begins to express the anger. Some children cry, sulk, talk, avoid or exhibit other physical or verbal behaviors, but very few children try to solve the problem or confront the issue. The third component is understanding the anger. This is where interpreting and evaluating takes place. Because children have limited abilities to reflect, adults need to guide children in understanding and managing feelings of anger. Children develop ideas about how to express emotions primarily through social interaction in their families and later by watching television, playing video games, and reading books. The following list helps you as a parent find ways to help guide your child's expression of anger:

✓ Learn to deal with your own and others' anger.
✓ Create a safe emotional climate (use clear, firm, flexible boundaries without shaming).
✓ Model responsible anger management.
✓ Help children develop self-regulatory skills.
✓ Encourage children to label feelings of anger and talk about it.
✓ Try to discover the reason for your child's anger and avoid shaming the child.
✓ Use books and stories about anger to help children understand and manage anger.

✓ Notice, compliment, reward appropriate anger management skills.
✓ Maintain open communication with your child.
✓ Teach understanding and empathy.

Anger is a very normal and healthy emotion. It is how you react to anger that makes it positive or negative. Children must know that even when they are angry, they are still responsible for behavior. Strategies for what to do with anger include: talk about it with someone who is good at listening, draw a picture of what your anger feels like, let yourself cry angry tears, hit a pillow or play with clay, take a walk, or write in a journal. Unhealthy responses to anger might include: hitting someone or using hurtful words, throwing things, running away, punching walls, giving the silent treatment, or lashing out at people (www.choa.org/brainstorm/anger.shtml).

I found interesting the stress-producing anger provocations most often faced by young children: conflict over possessions, physical assault, verbal conflict (teasing/taunting), rejection, and issues of compliance (www.athealth.com).

We wrapped up before Thanksgiving with learning some very important information about anger. Be sure to ask your child what they learned and share information. Some really great books to check out on this subject include:

✓ Don't Rant and Rave on Wednesday (children's book) by Adolph Moser
✓ Hot Stuff to Help Kids Chill Out: The Anger Management Book by Jerry Wilde
✓ A Volcano in My Tummy by Eliane Whitehouse
✓ Taming the Dragon in your Child by Meg Eastman
✓ Sticks and Stones by Scott Cooper

As always, if you have any questions or comments, please let me know. I am here to help. Look for new "What's the Issue?" information in January.

Sincerely,

Name

Title

La Fecha

Estimados Padres,

"Lo que es el Asunto" emocionaba muy hoy. Los niños estaban muy abiertos y aprendieron mucho acerca del a menudo, la emoción entendida mal de la cólera. Según investigar del www. athealth. la cólera de com tiene tres componentes. Primero, el niño tiene lo que se llama el estado emocional de la cólera, que es donde el niño comienza a sentirse que la frustración de una meta a se bloquear o necesita yendo inapropiada. El segundo, el niño comienza a expresar la cólera. Algún grito de niños, enfado, discurso, evita o exhibe otras conductas físicas o verbales, pero muy pocos niños tratan de resolver el problema o confrontar el asunto. El tercer componente entiende la cólera. Esto es donde interpretando y para evaluar sucede. Porque niños han limitado las habilidades de reflejar, los adultos necesitan indicar niños en la comprensión y manejar los sentimientos de la cólera. Los niños desarrollan las ideas acerca de cómo expresar las emociones principalmente por interacción social en sus familias y posterior mirando la televisión, jugando los juegos video, y leer los libros.

La lista siguiente lo ayuda como una maneras de hallazgo de padre a ayudar la guía su expresión de niño de la cólera:

✓ Aprenda a tratar con su propio y los otros' la cólera.

✓ Cree un clima emocional seguro (el uso vacía, la firma, las fronteras flexibles sin avergonzar).

✓ La administración responsable modelo de la cólera.

✓ Los niños de la ayuda desarrollan las habilidades auto-regulativos.

✓ Alente a niños a marcar los sentimientos de la cólera y discurso acerca de lo.

✓ La prueba para descubrir la razón para su cólera de niño y evitar avergonzar el niño.

✓ Los libros del uso y cuentos acerca de la cólera para ayudar a niños entienden y manejan la cólera.

✓ La nota, el cumplido, la recompensa apropia las habilidades de la administración de la cólera.

✓ Mantenga comunicación abierta con su niño.

✓ Enseñe entendiendo y la empatía.

La cólera es una emoción muy normal y sana. Es cómo usted reacciona para enojar eso lo hace positivo o negativo. Los niños deben saber que aún cuando ellos están enojados, ellos son todavía responsables de la conducta. Las estrategias para lo que hacer con la cólera incluye: discurso acerca de lo con alguien que es bueno en escuchar, dibuja un retrato de lo que su cólera se siente como, permitió que usted mismo llore las lágrimas enojadas, golpee una almohada o el juego con arcilla, tome una caminata, o escriba en un diario. Las respuestas poco sano para enojar quizás incluya: golpeando alguien o utilizando palabras dañosas, tirando las cosas, escapándose, dando un puñetazo paredes, dando el tratamiento silencioso, o azotando fuera en personas (www.choa.org/brainstorm/anger.shtml).

Encontré interesando las provocaciones de la cólera de énfasis-produciendo más a menudo encarado por niños jóvenes: el conflicto sobre la posesión, el asalto físico, el conflicto verbal (molestando/incitar), el rechazo, y los asuntos de la conformidad (www.athealth.com).

Enrollamos antes de la Acción de gracias con aprender alguna información muy importante acerca de la cólera. Esté seguro preguntar a su niño lo que ellos aprendieron y comparten información. Nuestro programa de la anti-violencia de la escuela, Segundo Paso, también administración de cólera de direcciones. Algunos libros realmente gran averiguar en este sujeto incluye:

✓ *Don't Rant and Rave on Wednesday* (children's book) by Adolph Moser

✓ *Hot Stuff to Help Kids Chill Out: The Anger Management Book* by Jerry Wilde

✓ *A Volcano in My Tummy* by Eliane Whitehouse

✓ *Taming the Dragon in your Child* by Meg Eastman

✓ *Sticks and Stones* by Scott Cooper

Como siempre, si usted tiene cualquiera pregunta o comenta, permitió por favor mí saber. Yo aquí deberé ayudar. Tenga un bendijo maravillosamente la temporada de Vacaciones. Busque nuevo "lo que Es el Asunto" información en enero.

Sinceramente,

Nombre

Titulo

Goal-setting

"The more you read, the more things you know. The more you learn, the more places you'll go."
—Dr. Seuss

Choose a book—

Amazing Grace
or
Oh The Places You'll Go

Make a poster to promote the book club.

DeDe Coffman

Goal-setting Agenda

I. Read one of the stories together. (5 minutes)

II. Group Discussion questions. (10 minutes)

III. Go over Goals notes. (5 minutes)

IV. Do "What a Start, What a Finish..." activity. (10 minutes)

V. Do either the "Stretching Out" or "Mission Impossible" activity. (10 minutes)

VI. Complete the Goal Action Contract. (5 minutes)

Send home parent letter

Remind about next book club

Draw for shirt

la meta-colocación

Asombrando la Gracia

María Hoffman

LOS OBJETIVOS:

- ✓ Defina lo que una meta es.
- ✓ Aprenda la importancia de la colocación de la meta.
- ✓ Describa características de la meta buena.
- ✓ Sepa la diferencia entre la meta a largo plazo y a corto plazo.
- ✓ "Puedo" pensando en vez de "puedo'T."
- ✓ Aprenda acerca de la conexión entre determinación perserverance y logro.

Las preguntas para la Discusión del Grupo

(Está listo para discutir estas preguntas con todo detalle y la acción experimenta relacionado a ellos.)

1. ¿Qué era la Gracia'la meta de s? ¿Pareció imposible?
2. ¿Qué dos cosas Agraciaron tiene eso la ayudó vence sus obstáculos?
3. ¿Cómo hizo los cuentos de la lectura e imaginar la Gracia de ayuda obtiene la parte?
4. ¿Qué era algunos de los pasos Agracian tomó para alcanzar su meta?
5. ¿Cómo trataron las personas la Gracia cuando ella fue revelada su meta? ¿Piensa usted que esto alentaba o desalentaba? ¿Por qué?
6. ¿Alcanzó la Gracia su meta?
7. ¿Cómo piensa usted que la Gracia sentía cuando ella alcanzó su meta?

(¡Empiece el pensamiento acerca de las metas que usted puede tener para usted mismo... y lo que usted se debe hacer alcanzarlos!)

Available in Spanish

Amazing Grace

Mary Hoffman

Goal-setting

OBJECTIVES:

- ✓ Define what a goal is.
- ✓ Learn the importance of goal setting.
- ✓ Describe characteristics of good goal.
- ✓ Know difference between long-term and short-term goal.
- ✓ "I can" thinking instead of "I can't."
- ✓ Learn about the connection between determination/perserverance and achievement.

Questions for Group Discussion

(Be ready to discuss these questions in detail and share experiences related to them.)

1. What was Grace's goal? Did it seem impossible?

2. What two things did Grace have that helped her overcome her obstacles?

3. How did reading stories and imagining help Grace get the part?

4. What were some of the steps Grace took to reach her goal?

5. How did people treat Grace when she was revealed her goal? Do you think this was encouraging or discouraging? Why?

6. Did Grace reach her goal?

7. How do you think Grace felt when she reached her goal?

Start thinking about goals you may have for yourself... and what you need to do to reach them!

establEciendo metas

Oh, Cuan Lejos Llegaras

Dr. Seuss

OBJETIVOS:

- ✓ Definir que es una meta.
- ✓ Aprender la importancia de establecer metas.
- ✓ Describir las caracteristicas de una buena meta.
- ✓ Saber la diferencia entre metas a largo y corto plazo.
- ✓ Pensamiento "Yo puedo" en lugar de "Yo no puedo."
- ✓ Aprender acerca de la conección entre determinación/perseverancia y logro.

Las preguntas para la Discusión del Grupo

(Está listo para discutir estas preguntas con todo detalle y la acción experimenta relacionado a ellos.)

1. ¿Cuál crees que es el mejor modo de conducirte? ¿Qué es una meta? ¿Tener una meta te ayuda a conducirte en el camino ó "calle"correcta?

2. ¿Cómo se siente cuando tienes mucho que hacer ó realizar y no sabes donde o como empezar? ¿Te pueden ayudar las metas a empezar y a lograr triunfos? ¿Cómo?

3. ¿Qué son metas a largo plazo? ¿Metas a corto plazo?

4. ¿Qué son obstaculos? ¿Cómo están relacionados metas y obstaculos?

5. ¿Qué pasa cuando no alcanzas una meta? ¿Renuncias ó aprendes y modificas tu meta? ¿Qué deberías hacer con los errores?

6. ¿Qué tipo de sensaciones podrías tener al empezar una meta? ¿Al alcanzar una meta?

7. ¿Qué tipo de características necesitas tener para alcanzar tus meta?

8. ¿Qué trata de decir Dr. Seuss cuando dice "La Vida es un Gran Acto de Equilibrio?" ¿Te ayudan las metas a balancearte? ¿Cómo?

Available in Spanish

Oh The Places You'll Go

Dr. Seuss

OBJECTIVES:

- ✓ Define what a goal is.
- ✓ Learn the importance of goal-setting.
- ✓ Describe characteristics of good goal.
- ✓ Know difference between long-term and short-term goal.
- ✓ "I can" thinking instead of "I can't."
- ✓ Learn about the connection between determination/perserverance and achievement.

Questions for Group Discussion

(Be ready to discuss these questions in detail and share experiences related to them.)

1. How do you think the best way to "steer" yourself is? What is a goal? Does having a goal help steer you down the right path or "street?"

2. How does it feel when you have lots to do or accomplish and you don't know where or how to start? Can goals help you get started and go places? How?

3. What are long term goals? Short term goals?

4. What are obstacles? How are goals and obstacles related?

5. What happens when you don't reach a goal? Do you quit or do you modify your goal and learn? What should you do with mistakes?

6. What kinds of feelings might you have when starting a goal? When reaching a goal?

7. What are some characteristics you need to have in order to reach your goals?

8. What does Dr. Seuss mean when he says "Life's a Great Balancing Act?" Do goals help you balance? How?

Notes About Goals

Goals + Action Steps = Success

➤ **It's important that I feel good about myself.**

➤ **Everyday I will write a positive statement about myself.**

G Go for your DREAMS.

O Open your mind to any possibility.

A Aim high.

L Look into your dreams creating ACTION STEPS.

S See yourself reaching your goal.

 DeDe Coffman

What a Start, What a Finish...

Objective: The students will learn about setting goals and seeing their dreams become reality.

Materials: Small jigsaw puzzle, stopwatch, roadmap, picture frames, paper, and pens or markers.

Procedure: Give all students 5 or 6 puzzle pieces face down until all pieces have been handed out. Don't let students see the front of the puzzle box and don't tell them what it is. Time the students in putting the puzzle together. It should be difficult for the students. Stop them in 2 or 3 minutes. Discuss how hard it was and what made it difficult.

Now take the puzzle pieces and hand them out again showing them the front of the box. Discuss what the puzzles are suppose to look like thoroughly. Give them time to guess where pieces go. Let them start putting the puzzle together and time them again. It should be much easier and take less time.

Talk about how much easier it is to complete the task when you know what you are working toward. Pull out a road map. Ask students what things they have to know before they planned a road trip on the map. (They would have to know where they are currently located and where they want to go). Could a trip be planned if they didn't know this? No! You would simply end up driving first in this direction, and then in that direction—never knowing where you were going or when you had arrived!

Explain that the same is true for life. If we are going to achieve, we must begin with a clear picture of what we want to achieve in our mind. This is why goal-setting is important. Tell students before we take off in life, we need to set goals. A famous saying is "You can't hit if you don't swing." Give students a picture frame and a sheet of paper the same size. Have them take a few minutes to figure out what they want to accomplish this year, in the next 5 years, and in the next 10 years. They can draw pictures or write these on the paper. Let students make the pictures nice and neat so that they can put them in the frame for their room. They could also come up with a theme or quote that means something to them. Capturing their visions on paper will make the goals more meaningful!

S-T-R-E-T-C-H-I-N-G O-U-T

Objective: Students will be able to describe the characteristics of a good goal, tell how setting goals help people to "stretch themselves", and set one short term (1 week) goal.

Materials: (per group of students) Equal parts of blue glitter glue and water, mixed well, a solution made of 1 1/3 cups warm water and 4 TSP. Borax, a clear large cup, a craft stick for stirring, paper towels.

Procedure:

1. Ask the students to explain what a goal is. Use a sports metaphor to illustrate. Once they have agreed upon a definition of a goal, tell them that there are some qualities that make up a good goal. Help them through discussion to come to understand that a good goal is measurable, has a time limit, is achievable, is very specific, personal, important to them, and so forth.

2. Explain that a goal is like a map—it gets you where you want to be. A good goal stretches you and helps you become better and better.

3. Make Goal Goop. Tell students that goop will help you to remember that a good goal stretches you and helps you achieve more and more. While we work on our goop, I want you to think of 2 goals for yourself that you want to achieve in the next week, one for school and one for self. For example, you might want to improve your Math test grade by 5 points over your last test, and you might want to exercise for at least 30 minutes per day. Both of these goals meet all the requirements of being good goals.

4. Have the glue and water mixed beforehand. Mix the Borax (laundry activator that softens water) solution with glue solution. Have Borax mixed beforehand too. The Borax solution will accommodate up to 2 cups of mixture.

5. After pouring the glue solution into the Borax solution, students should roll it around in the solution using a craft stick until it firms up.

6. Lift the goop out of the solution and knead it for 2-3 minutes until it is stretchy. As students stretch and play with goop, have them tell you what their goals are.

Mission Impossible

Objective: Students will carry out a fun activity to demonstrate to them that something they thought was impossible is really possible. Students will then brainstorm examples of things they can now do that they once thought were impossible, and discuss what they did that made the "impossible" possible.

Materials: 3 x 5 index card for each person, scissors, Impossible sheet, and questions.

Procedure:

1. Hold up the 3 x 5 index card. Say, "I'll bet I can put my head through a hole in this card." Take a hole punch, punch a hole in the card, and hold it up. "Will this work?" Then, cut a larger hole in the card. "Will this work?" After a few tries like this, ask the students, "Do you think it is possible for me to put my head through a hole in this card?"

2. Then say, "Wait! I have an idea!" Carefully fold the card in half lengthwise. Then, make 13 or any odd number partial cuts widthwise. (Make the first cut on the fold, then turn the card around and cut towards the fold, and so on. End each cut about 1/4 of an inch away from the edge of the card.

3. Very carefully open the card up, and cut down the center line, leaving the end sections intact.

4. Gently stretch the card as far as it will go and pull it over your head. (When this is done with a sheet of notebook paper, it is large enough to step through).

5. Ask the students, "Why did you think this was impossible? How did I make it possible?" The point is impossible can become possible if we try and try again and think of things in different ways.

The Opportunity to be Your Best

My long-term Goal

_____

(name what you want to accomplish in the next 10 years)

I am willing to

_____

(what you are willing to sacrifice)

Short-term action steps

(changes to to to accomplish goals)

Goal Requirements:

❑ Must be realistic and achievable
❑ Must be specific and measurable
❑ Must be relevant
❑ Must be time-limited
❑ Must have sacrifices
❑ Must have steps

1. _____

2. _____

3. _____

"A goal is your map to get you where you want to be."

_____

(date)   (signature)

Date

Dear Parents,

What's the Issue? was very productive today. I was so excited to help your child see the importance of goal setting in their life. When my youngest son came home from his first day in kindergarten, I asked him if he had learned very much that day. He replied, "Nah, I gotta go back again tomorrow." He was soon going to learn that most of life is a series of "going-back-agains." We all learn step-by-small step. Research has proved that it is a good idea to start talking about setting small, reachable goals when your children are fairly young, and to find ways to help them feel good about their accomplishments. Yesterday is considered experience and tomorrow is considered hope, but today is a great way for us to get from one place to another. Goal setting empowers children! They learn that they can have control over their learning. They can make things happen.

Establishing goals is imperative in this frenzied pace of modern life. We can show kids that goals teach us to sacrifice an immediate reward for a more satisfying future one. Even failed goals nudge us in the right direction. If we don't quite make it this time, we set more realistic expectations and go for it again. As our kids observe us sometimes succeeding and sometimes failing, they'll learn that it's okay to bump our heads and stub our toes occasionally, to be less than perfect. They will also come to understand that making mistakes in life usually provides remarkable opportunities to learn. No one needs to earn a blackbelt in goal setting; we only need to learn how to take baby steps that will eventually lead us toward our dreams and ideals.

Goal setting is a huge topic with much information. Children can set different kinds of goals: academic, process, and character. As well, it is easy for children to follow the S.M.A.R.T. goal setting pattern: specific, motivational, attainable, relevant, and trackable. It is also vital that children break their goals down into specific, smaller steps that will help them move up the goal success ladder. Some great websites with more information on children and goals are www.joshhind.com/goals, www.parentingwithdignity.com, mi.essortment.com/ideasteachgoal_rdzk.htm, www.focusonyourchild.com, and www.mochasofa.ca/family. If you have any questions or would like more information on this or other book club topics, please call me at school. Thanks for the opportunity to make a difference!

Sincerely,

Name

Title

La Fecha

Estimados Padres,

Qué es el Asunto era hoy muy productivo. Era tan emocionó a ayudar su niño ve la importancia de la colocación de la meta en su vida. Cuándo mi hijo más joven vino en casa de su primer día en el jardín de la infancia, yo lo pregunté si él había aprendido tanto ese día. El contestó, "Nah, yo gotta vuelve otra vez mañana." El pronto aprendería que la mayor parte de su vida es una serie de "going-back-agains." Todos aprendemos el paso por el paso pequeño. Investigación ha demostrado que es una idea buena empezar a hablar acerca de poner las metas pequeñas y accesibles cuando sus niños son bastante jóvenes, y para encontrar las maneras de ayudarlos se sienten bueno acerca de sus logros. Es considerado ayer la experiencia y se considera mañana la esperanza, pero es hoy una gran manera para el uso de obtener de un lugar a otro. ¡La colocación de la meta autoriza a niños! Ellos aprenden que ellos pueden tener el control sobre su aprender. Ellos pueden hacer las cosas suceden.

Establecer las metas son imprescindibles en este ritmo frenético de la vida moderna. Podemos mostrar los niños que metas nos enseñan a sacrificar una recompensa inmediata para un futuro más agradable uno. Las metas aún falladas nos dan un codazo en la dirección correcta. Si nosotros no exactamente lo hacemos esta vez, nosotros ponemos adn más práctico de esperanzas va para lo otra vez. Cuando nuestros niños nos observan que triunfando fallando a veces y a veces, ellos aprenderán que deberán golpear las cabezas y golpear los dedos ocasionalmente, para ser menos que perfeccionan. Ellos vendrán también entender que eso haciendo los errores en la vida proporcionan generalmente las oportunidades notables para aprender. Nadie necesita ganar un blackbelt en la colocación de la meta; nosotros sólo necesitamos aprender a cómo tomar a bebé los pasos que eventualmente nos dirigirán hacia nuestros sueños e ideales.

La colocación de la meta es un tema inmenso con mucha información. Los niños pueden poner las clases diferentes de metas: académico, el proceso, y el carácter. También, es fácil para niños para seguir el S.M.A.R.T. la pauta de la colocación de la meta: específico, motivador, accesible, pertinente, y trackable. Es también esencial que niños rompan sus metas hacia abajo en los pasos específicos y más pequeños que ayudarán ellos mueven arriba la escalera de éxito de meta. Algunos gran sitios web con más información en niños y metas son www.joshhind.com/goals, www.parentingwithdignity.com, miessortment.com/ideasteachgoal_rdzk.htm, www.focusonyourchild.com, and www.mochasofa.ca/family. Si usted tiene cualquiera pregunta o querría más información en este u otros temas de clubes de libro, por favor me llaman al colegio. ¡Da las gracias para la oportunidad de hacer una diferencia!

Sinceramente,

Nombre

Titulo

Goal Setting Quiz

Goal setting is a powerful skill that can enhance your child's chances of success in school and life. The good news is that goal setting is clearly a skill you can teach your child. Choose goals that are challenging, but within reach. The eight questions below will help you determine if the goal your child sets is reachable.

❑ He or she can clearly picture exactly what he or she wants to accomplish.

❑ This is something that he or she really wants to take responsibility for achieving.

❑ He or she has thought through all the steps necessary to succeed.

❑ He or she can explain the details of the plan to someone else.

❑ It makes sense for him or her to do this.

❑ He or she has all the necessary skills to achieve the goal.

❑ He or she has the necessary support to succeed.

❑ He/She has enough time to achieve the goal.

If all boxes are not checked, you might want to help your child rethink his or her goal.

DeDe Coffman

Manners

"Reading furnishes the mind only with materials for knowledge; it is thinking that makes what we read ours."

—John Locke

Choose a book—

The Thingumajig Book of Manners
or
Rude Mule

Make a poster to promote the book club.

Manners Agenda

   I. Read one of the stories suggested. (5 minutes)

  II. Group Discussion questions. (10 minutes)

 III. Discuss Table Manners for Children. (5 minutes)

 IV. Do You Have Something to Say activity. (10 minutes)

  V. Going to a Picnic activity. (10 minutes)

Send home parent letter

Remind about next book club

Draw for shirt

las maneras

The Thingamujig Book of Manners

Irene Keller

LOS OBJETIVOS:

- ✓ Los participantes definirán qué maneras son.
- ✓ Los participantes serán capaces de describer.
- ✓ Participantes buenos de maneras de mesa serán capaz de distinguirse entre lo que no es la conducta aceptable y aceptable con respecto a otros.
- ✓ Los participantes aprenderán la manera de hablar utilizando cortésmente las maneras verbales correctas.
- ✓ Los participantes serán dados la práctica y papel-jugando con maneras.

Las preguntas para la Discusión del Grupo

(Está listo para discutir estas preguntas con todo detalle y la acción experimenta relacionado a ellos.)

1. ¿Mostró el Thingumajigs las maneras buenas? ¿Por qué o por qué no?
2. ¿Es relacionada la salud buena a maneras buenas? ¿Cómo?
3. ¿Pueden afectar los hábitos de la salud de otros a personas alrededor de ellos? ¿Cómo?
4. ¿Qué era parte de las maneras malas del libro que necesitamos de recordar?
5. ¿Cómo reaccionan las personas a usted cuando usted se pone'T tiene las maneras buenas?
6. ¿Pueden ser relacionadas las maneras buenas a tiene éxito en la vida? ¿Cómo?

Manners

The Thingumajig Book of Manners

Irene Keller

OBJECTIVES:

- ✓ Participants will define what manners are.
- ✓ Participants will be able to describe good table manners.
- ✓ Participants will be able to distinguish between what is acceptable and not acceptable behavior in regards to others.
- ✓ Participants will learn the way to speak politely using correct verbal manners.
- ✓ Participants will be given practice and role-playing with manners.

Questions for Group Discussion

(Be ready to discuss these questions in detail and share experiences related to them.)

1. Did the Thingumajigs show good manners? Why or Why not?
2. Is good health related to good manners? How?
3. Can the health habits of others affect people around them? How?
4. What were some of the bad manners from the book that we need to remember?
5. How do people react to you when you don't have good manners?
6. Can good manners be related to being successful in life? How?

Mulo Grosero

Pamela Edwards

las maneras

LOS OBJETIVOS:

✓ Los participantes definirán qué maneras son.

✓ Los participantes serán capaces de describer.

✓ Participantes buenos de maneras de mesa serán capaz de distinguirse entre lo que no es la conducta aceptable y aceptable con respecto a otros.

✓ Los participantes aprenderán la manera de hablar utilizando cortésmente las maneras verbales correctas.

✓ Los participantes serán dados la práctica y papel-jugando con maneras.

Las preguntas para la Discusión del Grupo

(Está listo para discutir estas preguntas con todo detalle y la acción experimenta relacionado a ellos.)

1. ¿Mostró el mulo grosero las maneras buenas? ¿Por qué o por qué no?

2. ¿Qué hace la palabra grosero significa a usted? ¿Qué piensa usted cuándo personas son hablar groseras o grosero en su conducta?

3. ¿Es relacionada la salud buena a maneras buenas? ¿Cómo?

4. ¿Pueden afectar los hábitos de la salud de otros a personas alrededor de ellos? ¿Cómo?

5. ¿Qué era parte de las maneras malas del libro que necesitamos de recordar?

6. ¿Cómo reaccionan las personas a usted cuando usted se pone'T tiene las maneras buenas? ¿Ayuda a ignorar a personas cuando ellos se ponen'T tiene las maneras buenas? ¿Cómo podría ayudar cortésmente usted alguien quién doesn'T tiene las maneras buenas?

7. ¿Pueden ser relacionadas las maneras buenas a tiene éxito en la vida? ¿Cómo?

Available in Spanish

Manners

Rude Mule

Pamela Edwards

OBJECTIVES:

- ✓ Participants will define what manners are.
- ✓ Participants will be able to describe good manners.
- ✓ Participants will be able to distinguish between what is acceptable and not acceptable behavior in regards to others.
- ✓ Participants will learn the way to speak politely using correct verbal manners.
- ✓ Participants will be given practice and role-playing with manners.

Questions for Group Discussion

(Be ready to discuss these questions in detail and share experiences related to them.)

1. Did the rude mule show good manners? Why or Why not?
2. What does the word rude mean to you? What do you think when people are rude talking or rude in their behavior?
3. Is good health related to good manners? How?
4. Can the health habits of others affect people around them? How?
5. What were some of the bad manners from the book that we need to remember?
6. How do people react to you when you don't have good manners? Does it help to ignore people when they don't have good manners? How could you politely help someone who doesn't have good manners?
7. Can good manners be related to being successful in life? How?

Do You Have Something to Say?

Objective: Children will understand and use correct verbal manners and courteous expressions.

Materials: Manners game board and flower game pieces

Procedures: Discuss what manners are. Recognize all answers; paraphrase as necessary. Discuss that we have particular ways of talking to each other that are very mannerly. This is called being respectful or having good manners. Emphasize that this is just one type of manners. Discuss with students whether they like to be around someone who is respectful and courteous or someone unmannerly and rude. You can compare this type of atmosphere to being in a garden where beautiful flowers cover the dull grass and dirt. Explain that most disrespectful people don't care about others' feelings. Describe the "Manners Game" and how it works (students will put flowers on stems in a garden each time they role-play correctly how to be verbally polite). Scenarios are at the end of this lesson to put on the backs of cut out flowers. You also need a poster board that looks like a garden full of stems where children can place their cut out flowers. Children will read the situation on each flower and give students a chance to respond with the suitable phrase.

Scenarios: 1) Everyone in your art class is drawing and you get up to go show your teacher. Accidentally, you bump into your friend's table messing up his picture. 2) Your mother takes you with her to grandmother's house. Grandmother offers you oatmeal cookies, but you really don't like oatmeal cookies. 3) You are at Pizza Planet with your family. You have finished your pizza and are ready to go play games. 4) You give your teacher an apple because you think she's the best and she replies with "Thank you sweetie. You are super! 5) Your teacher gives you candy because you have finished all work for the week with no behavioral problems. 6) You are walking at school down the hall and as you turn a corner, you bump into someone coming the other way. 7) On the first day of school, your mother introduces you to your new teacher. 8) Your lunch didn't agree with you today and you accidentally pass gas during reading time. 9) Your mom made your favorite dish for dinner and you want a second helping. 10) You go to a family picnic with your family at dad's work. Your dad introduces you to his boss. 11) On the way to your class this morning, you see the principal and she says, "Good morning, how are you today?" 12) Your mother offers you seconds on dessert, but you are full. 13) Your family goes to visit your grandmother and she wants you to sing and play the piano for her senior friends. You don't think it will be much fun. 14) At lunch, your friend said that she wants you to come over. You think she said, "You look like Rover." 15) Your friend drops her ice cream on the floor at lunch. 16) You are trying to hear what the teacher is saying, but a paper airplane keeps flying over head causing you to not be able to hear what she is saying.

Going to a Picnic

Objective: Children will learn suitable dinner manners.

Materials: Red and white checkered table cloth, picnic basket, patterns for various food items with scenarios on back, picture or statue of a pig.

Procedures: Discuss why good table manners are important. What are the social implications of poor manners. Introduce the game. Explain that we are going to have a picnic on the red and white checkered table cloth. Our game starts at the picnic basket and ends when we get to "Eat 'em up Pig." Every student will have a turn to pick out a piece of food from the basket that will have a situation on the back. If the child responds to the situation with correct manners then they get to place the food on the table cloth for the picnic. If the response is incorrect, the food goes back into the basket to try again. When all food is out, the game is over and the picnic may begin. (You could also have some sort of snack ready for this game when it's over to hand out). Ideas for food items include: muffins, sandwiches, hotdogs, cheese, carrots, pizza, grapes, corn-on-the-cob, pie, and so forth.

Scenarios: 1) Eat em up Pig is having trouble getting her peas onto her spoon. 2) Eat em up Pig can feel juice from her corn-on-the-cob running down her chin. 3) Eat em up Pig's mother offers her some roast beef and she really wants some. 4) Eat em up Pig is eating macaroni and cheese with her fork. How should she hold her fork? 5) Eat em up Pig is finished with her meal. Where should she put her fork, spoon, and knife? 6) Eat em up Pig can't wait to tell Fatty Patty Pig about the new pig spa downtown, but she just took a big bite of green beans. 7) Eat em up Pig is eating in a nice restaurant. There are several forks lined up beside her plate. How does she know which fork to use first? 8) Eat em up Pig has finished her meal and is ready to leave the table. 9) Eat em up Pig has eaten all the cereal out of her bowl. All that is left is milk. What should she do? 10) Eat em up Pig is full, but there is still a little food on her plate. What should she do? 11) Eat em up Pig accidentally burped at the table. What should she say? 12) Eat em up Pig finished her meal in a fine restaurant. What should she do with her cloth napkin? 13) Eat em up Pig wants to use the salt and pepper, but she can't reach them without reaching over her neighbor's plate. 14) Eat em up Pig is ready to eat. What should she do with her napkin? 15) Eat em up Pig wants ketchup for her fries. What should she say? 16) Eat em up Pig is trying to decide on appropriate dinner conversation. She should tell the others at her table about what. 17) Eat em up Pig is eating lunch in the school cafeteria. After she has finished, what should she do?

Date

Dear Parents,

As adults, we often think that children should be able to just "pick up" manners. Not so! With many parents working and so much for children to learn, it is often hard to fit it all in. In any civilized society, there's a code of conduct all must learn whether that is at the dinner table, on the playground/work, or within a friendship. While today is definitely more casual than days past, children must still be conscious of their behavior and how that behavior fits into society.

Kids really enjoy learning the correct way to function in society. Whether they do it or not is another story. It is up to us to hold them accountable for what's important in our own individual families. FamilyFun.com offers some great information on manners. I found the nine tips for teaching manners extremely helpful. The website also gives the three areas to focus on: The Magic Words, Telephone Protocol, and Table Manners. If you would like to visit this website, just type in familyfun.com and search for teaching manners. I have also included on the back of this letter suggested table manners for children.

If you have any questions, please feel free to call me at school. I hope your child learned something helpful. Manners are important and the effect they have on others is significant.

Sincerely,

Name

Title

Table Manners for Children

✓ Wash hands before sitting down.

✓ Leave toys, books, and pets behind.

✓ Place the napkin in your lap when you sit down.

✓ Sit up straight and don't slouch.

✓ Ask politely for things to be passed. Never reach across the table.

✓ Wait until everyone is seated and served before starting to eat.

✓ Keep elbows off the table.

✓ Never chew with your mouth open.

✓ Never talk with your mouth full.

✓ Use utensils quietly without banging them.

✓ Keep your knife out of your mouth.

✓ Never play with food.

✓ Never grab food from other people's plates.

✓ Ask politely for seconds.

✓ Ask to be excused from the table.

✓ Clear your plate from the table and take it into the kitchen

Telephone Protocol

Use courtesy when answering the phone. Teach your children the following phone manners:

❏ Greet callers politely "Thank you for calling the Coffmans."

❏ Put the phone down quietly to go and tell someone in the house to pick up.

❏ If the person wanted is not there, ask "May I take a message."

❏ Assure the person you will take care of the message and thank them again for calling.

❏ Never tell callers you are home alone. If an adult is requested, simply say that the person cannot get to the phone right now. Never give your name to callers. Never give out any information about self or family including names or addresses.

❏ In emergencies, dial 9-1-1 for help and talk clearly.

La Fecha

Estimados Padres,

Cuando los adultos, nosotros a menudo pensamos que niños deben ser capaces "recoger" apenas las maneras. ¡No tan! Con muchos padres que trabajan y tanto para niños para aprender, a menudo duramente lo deberá quedar todo en. En alguna sociedad civilizada, hay un código de conducto todo debe aprender si eso está en la mesa de la cena, en el campo de juegos/trabajo, o dentro de una amistad. Mientras es hoy definitivamente más casual que el pasado de días, los niños deben ser todavía conscientes de su conducta y cómo eses ataques de conducta en la sociedad.

Los niños gozan realmente aprendiendo la manera correcta a funcionar en la sociedad. Si ellos lo hacen o no son otro cuento. Está hasta nosotros tenerlos responsable para lo que es importante en nuestras propias familias individuales. Familyfun.com ofertas alguna gran información en maneras. Encontré las nueve puntas para enseñar las maneras muy útil. El sitio web da también las tres áreas a enfocar en: las palabras mágicas, protocolo de teléfono, y las maneras de mesa. Si usted querría visitar este sitio web, apenas tipo en familyfun.com

Y la búsqueda para enseñar las maneras. He incluido también en la espalda de esta carta manenrs sugerido de mesa para niños.

Si usted tiene cualquiera pregunta, se siente por favor libre llamarme al colegio. Espero que su niño aprendiera algo útil. Las maneras son importantes y el efecto que ellos tienen en otros es significativo.

Sinceramente,

Nombre

Titulo

Posponga las Maneras para Niños

✓ Las manos del lavado sentándose antes.

✓ La hoja juguetea, los libros, y los animales favoritos atrás.

✓ Coloque la servilleta en su regazo cuando usted se sienta.

✓ Yérguese y póngase'T está repantigado.

✓ Pregunte cortésmente para cosas para ser pasado.

✓ Nunca alcance a través de la mesa.

✓ Espere hasta que todos sean sentados y son servidos antes empezar a comer.

✓ Mantenga codos de la mesa.

✓ Nunca masque con la boca abre.

✓ Nunca discurso con la boca repleta.

✓ Utilice útiles calladamente sin los golpear.

✓ Mantenga su cuchillo fuera de su boca.

✓ Nunca juego con alimento.

✓ Nunca alimento de agarro de otras personas's chapa.

✓ Pregunte cortésmente por segundos.

✓ Pida ser dispensado de la mesa.

✓ Claro su plato de la mesa y lo toma en la cocina.

Protocolo telefonico

Use cortesía cuando conteste el teléfono. Enseñe a sus hijos los siguientes modales al contestar el teléfono:

❏ Saluden cortésmente a los que llamen "Gracias por llamar a los Coffmans"

❏ Baja el teléfono en silencio para ir a llamar a quien le hablan

❏ Si no está la persona a la que llaman, pregunta "Puedo tomar el mensaje."

❏ Asegura a la persona que pasaras el mensaje y agradecele otra vez por llamar.

❏ Nunca le digas a nadie que estás solo en la casa. Si requieren un adulto, simplemente di que la persona no puede contester el teléfono en ese momento. Nunca des tu nombre a los que llamen. Nunca des ninguna información acerca de ti mismo ó de tu familia incluyendo nombres ó direcciones.

❏ En emergencias, para pedir ayuda marca 9-1-1 y habla claramente.

Friendship

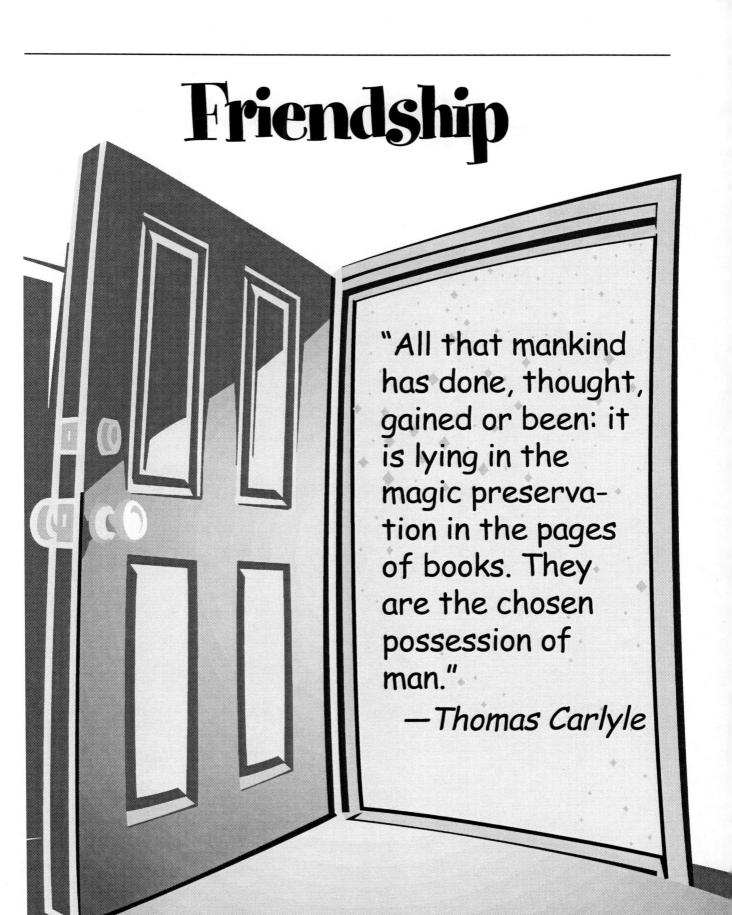

"All that mankind has done, thought, gained or been: it is lying in the magic preservation in the pages of books. They are the chosen possession of man."

—Thomas Carlyle

Choose a book—

The Grouchy Ladybug
or
Que le pasa a Timmy

Make a poster to promote the book club.

Friendship Agenda

For the last book club meeting, I have a pizza party because at the end, we talk about making friendship pizza. The children get to eat pizza while they work on their Friendship Pizza. I invite parents to join us a little early to help their child with their friendship pizza as well as their action plan. I also wear an apron and chef hat to make it more memorable. (Inviting the parents helps them to really understand what happens in book club.)

    I. Read one of the stories together. (5 minutes)
   II. Group Discussion questions. (10 minutes)
 III. 20 Ways to Make Other Feel Special. (5 minutes)
 IV. Make Friendship Pizza. (10 minutes)
  V. Discuss Friendship Action Plan. (5 minutes)

Send home parent letter
Remind about next year's book club
Draw for shirt

la amistad

La Mariquita Malhumorada

Eric Carle

LOS OBJETIVOS:

- ✓ Los participantes aprenderán características de un amigo bueno.
- ✓ Los participantes identificarán lo que hace a amigos malos.
- ✓ Los participantes se distinguirán entre amigos buenos y malos.
- ✓ Los participantes definirán lo que es importante a ellos en una amistad.
- ✓ Los participantes encontrarán áreas débiles de amistad para trabajar en.

Las preguntas para la Discusión del Grupo

(Está listo para discutir estas preguntas con todo detalle y la acción experimenta relacionado a ellos.)

1. La mariquita malhumorada fue ruda con la mariquita amigable. ¿Te hubiera gustado estar cerca de la mariquita amigable o de la malhumorada? ¿Por qué?

2. ¿Cómo se supone que los amigos deben tratarse uno al otro? ¿Qué tipo de cosas los amigos deberían hacer uno por el otro?

3. ¿Le permitió la mariquita amigable a la mariquita malhumorada que la tratara mal? ¿Cómo amigos es importante apoyarnos a nosotros mismos y no dejar que otros nos dominen?

4. ¿La mariquita malhumorada encontró muchos insectos y animals, pero no fue amable con ninguno de ellos? ¿Por qué crees que ella no fue amistosa? ¿Cuáles serán algunas razones por las cuales la gente no es amigable o es malhumorada? ¿Cómo deberíamos tratarlos?

5. ¿Cómo somos tratados cuando no somos un buen amigo? ¿Quiere la gente estar cerca de nosotros? ¿Qué características son importantes que tengamos para ser un buen amigo?

6. Al final del cuento, la mariquita amigable le ofrece algunos áfidos a la mariquita malhumorada otra vez. ¿Crees que perdonar es importante en una amistad? ¿Habrá tiempos en que no seamos un buen amigo? ¿Que deberíamos hacer cuando eso suceda?

Available in Spanish

The Grouchy Ladybug

Eric Carle

OBJECTIVES:

- ✓ Participants will learn characteristics of a good friend.
- ✓ Participants will identify what makes bad friends.
- ✓ Participants will distinguish between good and bad friends.
- ✓ Participants will define what is important to them in a friendship.
- ✓ Participants will find weak friendship areas to work on.

Questions for Group Discussion

(Be ready to discuss these questions in detail and share experiences related to them.)

1. The grouchy ladybug was rude to the friendly ladybug. Would you have wanted to be around the friendly ladybug or the grouchy one? Why?

2. How are friends suppose to treat each other? What types of things should friends do for each other?

3. Did the friendly ladybug allow the grouchy ladybug to bully her or run over? As a friend is important to stick up for ourselves and not let others dominate us?

4. The grouchy ladybug came upon many different bugs and animals, but she wasn't nice to any of them? Why do you think she was unfriendly? What might be some reasons for why people are unfriendly or grouchy? How should we treat them?

5. How do we get treated when we are not a good friend? Do people want to be around us? What characteristics are important for us to have in order to be a good friend?

6. At the end of the story, the friendly ladybug offered some aphids to the grouchy ladybug again. Do you think forgiveness is important in a friendship? Are there going to be times when we are not a good friend? What should we do when that happens?

la amistad

Que le pasa a Timmy

Maria Shriver

LOS OBJETIVOS:

- ✓ Define la amistad
- ✓ Discute los tipos diferentes de amistades.
- ✓ Discute cómo prejuicio o stereotyping afectan las amistades.
- ✓ Contesta la pregunta de "propósito" y cómo que relaciona a personas's vive.
- ✓ Contesta la pregunta de "propósito" y cómo que relaciona a personas's vive.
- ✓ Contesta la pregunta de "propósito" y cómo que relaciona a personas's vive.

Las preguntas para la Discusión del Grupo

(Está listo para discutir estas preguntas con todo detalle y la acción experimenta relacionado a ellos.)

1. ¿Qué es la amistad?

2. Hay muchos tipos diferentes de amistades como mejores amigos, los conocidos, etc. ¿Cuántos tipos diferentes de amistades tiene usted? ¿Quién es las personas en sus círculos de amigos? ¿Quién es su mejor amigo? ¿Por qué? ¿Qué es la diferencia entre mejores amigos, amigos buenos, y los conocidos?

3. En el libro, Kate advirtió Timmy en el campo de juegos, pero pensó él pareció de algún modo diferente de ella. ¿Piensa usted que personas pueden ser amigos con personas que son diferentes de ellos? ¿Qué quizás sea algunos desafían estas amistades? ¿Qué quizás sea algunas ventajas a son amigos con alguien que es un poco diferente de usted?

4. ¿Kate preguntó a su mamá la pregunta, "Qué'?" Hace la injusticia de s con lo Timmy piensa ayudaría a pensar no tanto acerca de "lo que'la injusticia de s" con personas como "lo que'el derecho de s" con personas? ¿Por qué?

5. ¿Por qué piensa usted que personas obtienen nervioso alrededor de personas que son diferentes? ¿Cómo debe manejarse usted alrededor de personas que son diferentes?

6. ¿Cómo usted piensa que Timmy sentía cuándo saludó lo Kate? ¿Cómo piensa usted que Kate sentía acerca de ella misma? ¿Lo tenido estuvo jamás nervioso al encontrar a un amigo nuevo? ¿Cómo lo manejó usted?

7. ¿Qué es el valor? ¿Toma el valor para defender a a personas que son diferentes?

8. ¿Era Kate un amigo bueno a Timmy? ¿Cómo sabe usted? ¿Qué características componen a un amigo bueno? ¿Qué tal un amigo malo?

9. En el libro, Kate'mamá de s la dice que todos una tierra está aquí para una razón. ¿Cree usted esto?

10. ¿Qué una cosa piensa usted toda necesidad de personas más que nada más en una relación? ¿Piensa usted que el sentimiento aceptado es importante? ¿Cómo lo afecta? Describa a un socio un tiempo usted sentía aceptado y un tiempo que usted hizo'T se siente como usted perteneció?

Available in Spanish

Friendship

What's Wrong with Timmy?

Maria Shriver

OBJECTIVES:

- ✓ Define friendship.
- ✓ Discuss the different types of friendship.
- ✓ Understand how prejudice or stereotyping can affect relationships in a person's life and friendships.
- ✓ Learn the characteristics of a good friend and bad friend.
- ✓ Discuss importance of acceptance.

Questions for Group Discussion

(Be ready to discuss these questions in detail and share experiences related to them.)

1. What is friendship? What words come to mind when you think of the word friendship?

2. There are many different types of friendship like best friends, acquaintances, etc. How many different types of friendships do you have? What people are in your circle of friends? Who is your best friend? Why? What is the difference between best friends, good friends, and acquaintances?

3. In the book, Kate notices that Timmy is different than the other children? Do you think people can be friends with people who are different than them? What could be some challenges in a relationship where two friends are different? What could be some advantages in a relationship where two friends are different?

4. Kate asked her mom a question about what's wrong with Timmy. Do you think that you can be friends with someone who is disabled? Why or Why not? Do you think that you can learn things from everyone no matter what their challenges?

5. Why do you think that people are nervous around people who are different? How should you act around people who are different?

6. How do you think Timmy felt when Kate greeted him? Do you think Kate felt the same way? Why or Why not? How does it feel when we befriend someone? Do you get nervous when you have to find a new friend? Is it hard for you? Why?

7. What is courage? Does it take courage to defend someone who is different?

8. Was Kate a good friend to Timmy? What are some characteristics of a good friend? What are some characteristics of a bad friend?

9. In the book, Kate's mother tells her that each of us is here for a reason. Do you believe this to be true? Should we look for what people can do instead of what they can't do?

10. What do you think is the most important thing that people need in a relationship? Do you think acceptance is important? How does feeling accepted make you feel? Describe a situation when you felt accepted and one when you didn't feel accepted?

The Grouchy Ladybug & Friendship

Objective: Students will learn characteristics of a friend.

Materials: *The Grouchy Ladybug* by Eric Carle, paper ladybugs with good and bad friendship characteristics (you could also catch some ladybugs and allow students to look at them—making sure they are not hurt and then release them after the activity.)

Procedures: After reading one of the books, explain that some of the ladybugs do things that attract friends and others do things that keep friends away. Tell the children that the ones who attract friends will be hung on the wall and the ones who don't will be separated. Sort through ladybugs with students orally. After completing the activity, if you have real ladybugs, go outside and release them. You could symbolize the release as what we have to do with friends sometimes in allowing them to make other friends or that this is a new beginning to us all being better friends.

Friendship/Unfriendly characteristics:

✓ I get into trouble at school.

✓ I am bossy.

✓ Others get to decide what we play.

✓ When I get mad at someone, I try to make everyone else mad at that person too.

✓ I tattle.

✓ I can only have one friend at a time.

✓ I call people names.

✓ I tease and bully people.

✓ I am angry a lot.

✓ I brag about my achievements.

✓ I play unfairly.

✓ When I make a new friend, I don't play with my old friends anymore.

✓ I hit and kick others.

✓ I whine.

✓ I look for good in everyone.

✓ I'm a good listener.

✓ I do nice things for others.

✓ I'm honest and fair.

✓ I smile a lot and look for positives.

✓ I let people know that I care about them.

✓ I respect others and their things.

✓ I say I'm sorry when I am wrong.

✓ I cooperate with others.

DeDe Coffman

20 Ways to Make Others Feel Special

✓ Ask them to play with you.

✓ Ask them what they would like to play.

✓ Let them know when you like their ideas.

✓ Let them go first.

✓ Play fair.

✓ Be a good sport.

✓ Share things with them.

✓ Offer to help them.

✓ Let them borrow something.

✓ Be honest.

✓ Help them feel better when they make mistakes.

✓ Stick up for them.

✓ Do them a favor expecting nothing in return.

✓ Listen.

✓ Encourage.

✓ Give compliments.

✓ Keep secrets and promises.

✓ Apologize and ask for forgiveness when needed.

✓ Give forgiveness.

✓ Let them have other friends.

✓

✓

✓

✓

✓

✓

✓

✓

✓

Making Friendship Pizza

Objective: Help children understand characteristics of being a good friend and bad friend and use language to enhance friendship.

Materials: Pizza boxes, dough cutouts (brown circles), toppings cutouts (red smaller circles with dots), trash can. (I've also used this for an end of year party and had actual pizza after.)

Procedure: Discuss friendship and the characteristics of being a bad and good friend. Tell students that we will make friendship pizza. Show them the toppings (pepperoni) with comments. Let them know that not all toppings are good. Some have spoiled just as friendships are often spoiled by things we say. We need to throw the "spoiled" pepperoni in the trash can and put the good pepperoni on the pizza. Give students individuals pizza cutouts that are glued inside pizza boxes and toppings. Have them work individually on their pizza. After students complete making their pizza, discuss the activity and comments. Role-play any difficult scenarios and have students take pizzas home. After finishing the activity, students can have real pizza party.

(Another version of this would be to let students actually make the pizzas by bringing all ingredients and putting them together. They make plug-in pizza cookers now.)

Comments: "I'll go get it for you."

"Mine's better than yours."

"It's O.K....I know you didn't mean to."

"I'll help you clean up."

"I can do it better than you."

"What would you like to do?"

"Want to play ball with me?"

"Bug off!"

"Don't touch it... It's mine!"

"I like your ideas."

"I'm sorry!"

"Me first. Me first."

"Don't feel bad... your getting better at it."

"Do it my way or I won't play."

"Get lost!"

"We don't want you to play."

"I made this for you."

"Want to borrow mine?"

DeDe Coffman

My Friendship Action Plan

I'm already good at...

_____
_____
_____
_____

I could be a little better at...

_____
_____
_____

One thing I will start doing to make others feel special is...

_____
_____
_____

Name_____ **Date**_____

Dear Parents,

Friendship is an important part of children's lives. We all need to feel acceptance. This is a basic need according to Maslow's hierarchy of needs. Working out peer relationships is an important part of school-age years. Children's friendships do more than provide them with playmates today—they are key building blocks for children's development and adjustment as adults. Friendships, for example, help children learn social skills, problem-solving skills and self-confidence.

Loving and nurturing family relationships give children a good foundation for moving out into the social world. Other ways parents can help children navigate peer relations include:

- ✓ Providing opportunities for children to socialize.
- ✓ Respecting your child's individuality.
- ✓ Talking with your child about social situations and their feelings and experiences.
- ✓ Letting your children and friends solve conflicts themselves.
- ✓ Talking to your school counselor if you are concerned.

We are all in this together, and it is up to us, as adults, to model how relationships are built and maintained. A great website for ways to help with children's friendships is www.ymca.net/programs/family/ptfriends.htm. There are also many great books out there. If you have any questions or need to talk, please give me a call.

Sincerely,

Name

Title

La Fecha

Estimados Padres,

La amistad es una parte importante de niños's vive. Todos nosotros necesidad de sentirse la aceptación. Esto es una necesidad básica según Maslow'la jerarquía de s de necesidades. Trabajar fuera relaciones de igual es una parte importante de años de escuela-edad. Los niños'las amistades de s hacen más que los proporcionan con compañeros hoy —they es componentes claves para niños'el desarrollo de s y ajuste como adultos. Las amistades, por ejemplo, ayudan a niños aprenden las habilidades sociales, las habilidades de resolución de problemas y confianza en sí mismo.

Adorar y nutrir las relaciones de la familia les dan a niños una base buena para mudar en el mundo social. Otros padres de maneras pueden ayudar a niños navegan las relaciones de igual incluyen:

- ✓ Proporcionar las oportunidades para niños para socializar.
- ✓ El respeto su niño'individualidad de s.
- ✓ Hablar con su niño acerca de situaciones sociales y sus sentimientos y acerca de las experiencias.
- ✓ Permitir sus niños y a amigos resuelven los conflictos sí mismos.
- ✓ Hablar a su consejero de la escuela si usted es concernido.

Somos todo en esto juntos, y estamos hasta nosotros, como los adultos, para modelar cómo relaciones se construyen y son mantenidas. Un gran sitio web para maneras de ayudar con niños'las amistades de s son www.ymca.net/programs/family/ptfriends.htm. Hay también muchos gran libros fuera allí. Si usted tiene cualquiera pregunta o necesita hablar, complacer me da una llamada.

Sinceramente,

Nombre

Titulo

Self-esteem

"I am somebody. I am me. I like being me. And I need nobody to make me some-body."

—Louis L'Amour

Choose a book—

I Knew You Could
or
Just the Way You Are

Make a poster to promote the book club.

Self-esteem Agenda

   I. Read the book with participants. (5 minutes)

  II. Go over group discussion questions. (10 minutes)

 III. Complete "It's Really Me" activity. (10 minutes)

 IV. Complete "Accentuate the Positive" activity. (15 minutes)

Send home parent letters

Remind about next book club

Draw for shirt

I Knew You Could

Craig Dorfman

Autoestima

OBJETIVOS:

- ✓ Los participantes empezarán a refleccionar en si mismos.
- ✓ Los participantes verán como encajan en el mundo (el gran panorama).
- ✓ Los participantes examinaran fortalezas y debilidades.
- ✓ Los participantes serán alentados a ser ellos mismos.
- ✓ Los participantes discutirán como la seguridad afecta nuestro camino por la vida.

Las preguntas para la Discusión del Grupo

(Está listo para discutir estas preguntas con todo detalle y la acción experimenta relacionado a ellos.)

1. ¿Cuáles son algunas "cosas" buenas y malas que atravesamos en la vida? ¿Estas cosas malas nos hacen sentir desanimados y como que no estamos bien? ¿Cómo? (ejemplos—perder un juego o amigo, molestar, etc.)

2. ¿Es importante sentirnos seguros de nosotros mismos como la pequeña locomotora? ¿Cómo te hace actuar y comportarte la seguridad? ¿Te tienes que sentir siempre bien y confiado o hay tiempos cuando no nos sentimos bien acerca de nosotros? ¿Cómo nos "golpeamos" algunas veces?

3. ¿Cuándo ves a otra gente, algunas veces deseas ser más como ellos? ¿Crees que a veces la gente te mira y desea eso? ¿Es difícil ser alguien que no eres? ¿Por qué o por qué no?

4. ¿Cómo sabes que estás en la dirección correcta en tu vida? ¿Cómo afectan tu vía tus fortalezas y debilidades?

5. ¿Está bien que sucedan los errores y y los "tuneles obscuros?" ¿Cómo puedes usar errores para salir de tuneles obscuros en la vida?

6. Si la vida es una travesía, cuáles son algunas cosas que deberíamos aprender en el camino? ¿Está bien apoyarnos en otros durante el trayecto?

7. ¿Es importante ser determinado en nuestra travesía y confiar en nosotros mismos? ¿Por qué ó por qué no?

8. ¿Cuál es una lección que has aprendido acerca de ti mismo y como encajas en el mundo en tu travesía? (Piensa acerca de una ocasión en que hiciste algo muy bueno ó algo no muy bueno)

9. Nombra 3 personas diferentes y discute una fortaleza y una debilidad en ellos ya que todos tenemos ambas.

Self-esteem

I Knew You Could

Craig Dorfman

OBJECTIVES:

- ✓ Participants will begin to reflect on self.
- ✓ Participants will look at how they fit into the world (the bigger picture).
- ✓ Participants will examine strengths and weaknesses.
- ✓ Participants will be encouraged to be themselves.
- ✓ Participants will discuss how confidence affects our life journey.

Questions for Group Discussion

(Be ready to discuss these questions in detail and share experiences related to them.)

1. What are some of the good and bad "stuff" we go through in life? Does this bad stuff make us feel discouraged and like we're not okay? How? (examples—losing a ball game or friend, teasing, and so forth)

2. Is it important to feel confident about ourselves like the little engine? How does confidence make you act and behave? Do you always have to be confident and feel okay or are there times when we feel not so good about ourselves? How do we "beat ourselves up" sometimes?

3. When you look around at other people, do you ever wish you were more like them? Do you think other people ever look at you and wish that? Is it hard to be someone that you're not? Why or why not?

4. How do you know that you're on the right track in your life? How do your strengths and weaknesses affect your track?

5. Are mistakes and "dark tunnels" okay to happen? How can you use mistakes to help you come out of dark tunnels in life?

6. If life is a journey, what are some of the things we should be learning along the way? Is it okay to lean on others along the way?

7. Is it important to be determined in our journey and trust in ourselves? Why or Why not?

8. What is one lesson you have learned about yourself and who your are and how you fit into the world so far on your journey? (Think about a time where you really did something great or something not so great)

9. Name 3 different people and discuss one strength in them and one weakness because we all have both.

Autoestima

Somos como Somos

Marcus Pfister

OBJETIVOS:

- ✓ Los participantes definirán autoestima.
- ✓ Los participantes discutirán la importancia de una buena autoestima.
- ✓ Los Participantes verán como la autoestima afecta las decisions y la vida de las personas.
- ✓ Los participantes discutirán los pasos para aumentar la autoestima.

Las preguntas para la Discusión del Grupo

(Está listo para discutir estas preguntas con todo detalle y la acción experimenta relacionado a ellos.)

1. En el libro Tal Como Tú Eres, todos los animales desearon ser como alguien más. ¿Alguna vez has desado ser como alguien más? ¿Por qué? ¿Alguna vez has tratado de ser como alguien más? ¿Cómo fue? ¿Cómo te sentiste?

2. ¿Por qué piensas que queremos ser como alguien más? ¿Crees que todos batallan para aceptar una parte de ellos mismos?

3. ¿Qué cosas haces que pueden causar que tengas baja autoestima?

4. Autoestima tiene mucho que ver con pensamientos negativos. Se ha dicho, "Negatividad genera Negatividad..." En el cuento, cada vez que un animal dijo algo que quería cambiar acerca de sí mismo, el próximo animal empezaba a no gustarle algo de ellos mismos. ¿Crees que la negatividad se contagia?

5. ¿Cómo te hace sentir cuando alguien te alienta ó admira como los animals hicieron al final del cuento?

6. ¿Qué significa "estar conforme con lo que tienes?"

7. ¿Crees que haya un propósito para cada quien en la vida? ¿Por qué ó por qué no?

8. ¿Cómo afecta la autoestima la vida de la gente? ¿Tenían los animales buena autoestima? ¿Por qué o por qué no? Escogiendo enfocarse en lo que no tenían, casi perdieron la oportunidad de divertirse estando todos juntos en una fiesta. ¿Crees que pensar bien acerca de ti mismo es una elección? ¿Circunstancias en tu vida (ser pobre, no tener muchos amigos, reprobar un examen, etc.) afecta la autoestima? ¿Cómo?

9. ¿Qué crees que la gente realmente admira en otra gente? Explica. ¿Tiene alguien la abilidad de poner estas cosas en práctica en su vida?

10. ¿Viene la autoestima de adentro o de afuera.

Available in Spanish

Just the Way You Are

Marcus Pfister

OBJECTIVES:

✓ Participants will define self-esteem.

✓ Participants will discuss the importance of good self-esteem.

✓ Participants will look at how self-esteem affects people's lives and decisions.

✓ Participants will discuss steps to enhancing self-esteem.

Questions for Group Discussion

(Be ready to discuss these questions in detail and share experiences related to them.)

1. In Just the Way You Are, the animals all wished they were like someone else. Have you ever wished you were like someone else? Why? Have you ever tried to be like someone else? How did that turn out? How did it make you feel?

2. Why do you think we want to be like someone else? Do you think everyone struggles with accepting some part of theirself?

3. What kinds of things do you do that might cause you to have lower self-esteem?

4. Self-esteem has much to do with negative thinking. It has been said, "Negativity breeds negativity..." In the story, each time an animal stated something that he wanted to change about himself, the next animal begin to not like something about themselves. Do you negativity is contagious?

5. How does it make you feel when someone encourages or admires you like the animals did at the end of the story?

6. What does it mean "to be content with what you have?"

7. Do you think that there is a purpose for everyone's life? Why or why not?

8. How does good self-esteem affect people's lives? Did the animal's have good self-esteem? Why or why not? By choosing to focus what they didn't have, they almost missed out on having a great time being together at a party. Do you think thinking good about yourself is a choice? Do circumstances in your life (being poor, not having many friends, failing a test, and so forth) affect self-esteem? How?

9. What do you think people really admire in other people? Explain. Does everyone have the ability to put these things into practice in their life?

10. Does self-esteem come from the inside or outside?

It's Really Me!!!

Objective: The students will learn about who they are and their unique makeup that makes them distinct individuals full of value.

Materials: Old magazines, poster paper, markers, glue, scissors, ink pad, photocopies of 5 general fingerprints (from encyclopedia).

Procedure: Begin by helping all students to press their thumbs on an ink pad and place their thumbprint onto the poster paper in the middle. Then show the students the photocopies of the five general fingerprints out of the encyclopedia. Have students try to identify which one theirs most closely matches. Discuss how different all fingerprints are and how that is evidence of our uniqueness. Tell them we were created different for a purpose so that we can all bring something special to the world to make it work! Only they have the unique fingerprint they do to make an imprint on the world like only they can make!

After talking about self-esteem, pass out old magazines and lead students into reflecting on who they are including likes/dislikes, strengths/weaknesses, heroes, goals, dreams, physical characteristics, behaviors, feelings, careers, places they've been, family and so forth. Allow students some time to think and write some cue words on the board. Next give every student poster paper or construction paper and explain that they are going to create a collage of who they are by cutting out pictures from the magazines that reveal around their thumbprint on the poster. Last students should put their name on the backs of the posters.

Hang the posters around the room and have students try to identify what poster belongs to who. Encourage them to find out about one another and compliment each other's uniqueness and individuality. Have the class discuss how each person is important to the world and what they can add based on their collages.

Accentuate the Positive

Objective: To help students verbalize positive traits about other people using that encouragement to build other's up as well as emphasis that all people bring different strengths to the world.

Materials: Pens or pencils, markers, paper with each student's name written on it in a downward direction (see example) or computer lab.

Procedure: Have the students create an acrostic with their name by using words that describe themselves. They can make their acrostic colorful and creative. You can even bring decorative supplies to decorate their acrostics. Give each student plenty of room to work on this privately within the group. Hopefully, each student will be able to reflect upon themselves and their worth. You could also do this part of the activity in the computer lab to utilize technology skills.

Next take up all acrostics and one by one, have student stand in front of the group so that students can tell each other positive characteristics that they see about their peers. Go around and as each student stands, let everyone give one strength or gift that they see about the person standing. You need to set the rules for this sharing and make sure that students know we are only talking about strengths. Help students to comment on behavior instead of physical characteristics. Record each positive comment at the bottom of the acrostics so students will have to take home.

D Driven

e Eager

D Dedicated

e Evolving

Others say I am...

1) _____

2) _____

3) _____

Date

Dear Parents,

A student enters school as a distinctive individual, shaped by genes, environment, and a certain glow within himself. An increased awareness of how extraordinary that matchless spark really makes him helps that student preserve that quality when the pressure is on to follow the crowd. My goal as a counselor is not to fabricate cookie-cutter children but to feed each student's individual spirit. An ancient Chinese proverb says, "I hear and I forget, I see and I remember, and I do and I understand."

As children we are all required to learn who we are in the world. And as we learn who we are, we learn to value and sometimes devalue portions of ourselves. For example we all get messages about our bodies, our minds, our feelings and our behaviors. It's from these messages that we build our awareness of self-esteem. Who we are in the world is not information we're born with. It's something we acquire. The experiences we have, and in response the beliefs we develop, establish our view of how we fit into the world. We all learned this lesson of self-valuing (or devaluing) by being in [relationship] to the world, it's essentials, and the people inhabiting it.

Self-esteem can be defined as how people feel about themselves. Children's levels of self-esteem are evident in their behavior and attitudes. If children feel good about themselves, these good feelings will be reflected in how they relate to friends, teachers, siblings, parents, and others. Self-esteem is something that affects individuals throughout life, therefore, it is very important for parents to help their children develop healthy levels of self-esteem. There are many things parents can do to help their children learn that they are lovable, capable, and competent, beginning when their children are at a very young age. Unfortunately, it is also at a very young age that children can begin to develop low self-esteem. Parents must be very careful not to plant the seeds of low self-esteem in their children unknowingly. The following guidelines help foster positive self-esteem:

- ✓ No Comparing (look at each child as a unique contribution accepting the child for who they are not who you want them to be).
- ✓ Realistic Expectations (set goals for your child based on who they are and where they fit into life developmentally).
- ✓ Freedom for Mistakes (don't encourage perfectionism and help children to become problem solvers who use mistakes as stepping stones).
- ✓ Opportunities for Success (create times for children to be successful by helping them break things into simple steps and setting them up for their strengths).
- ✓ Encourage (praise children for effort and doing their best instead of being the best; use positive self talk and discuss strengths).
- ✓ Accept children's unpleasant feelings (all feelings are accepted; talk about them and discuss how behavior is related to the person).
- ✓ Give choices (this creates ownership and responsibility).
- ✓ Give responsibilities and expect cooperation (never do for children what they can do for themselves).
- ✓ Keep a sense of humor (encourage children to see the bright side and laugh about themselves).

On the back of this letter, I have included "50 Things Parents Can Say to Children to Encourage and Praise Them." I hope that you find these suggestions from the Center for Effective Parenting helpful.

Sincerely,

Name

Title

Fifty Things Parents Can Say to Their Children to Praise and Encourage Them

1. You're on the right track now!
2. You're doing a great job!
3. Now you've figured it out!
4. That's RIGHT!
5. Now you have the hang of it!
6. That's the way!
7. Now you have it!
8. Nice going.
9. You did it that time!
10. GREAT!
11. FANTASTIC!
12. TREMENDOUS!
13. TERRIFIC!
14. How did you do that?
15. That's better.
16. EXCELLENT!
17. That's the best thing you've ever done.
18. Good going!
19. That's really nice.
20. WOW!
21. Keep up the good work.
22. Much better!
23. Good for you!
24. SUPER!
25. You do such a good job of ____.
26. You make it look easy.
27. Way to go!
28. You're getting better every day.
29. WONDERFUL!
30. I knew you could do it!
31. You're doing beautifully.
32. That's the way to do it!
33. Keep on trying.
34. You're the best!
35. You're doing much better today.
36. Keep working on it, you're getting better.
37. You're very good at that.
38. I'm very proud of you.
39. I like the way you listen.
40. You've just about got it.
41. You can do it.
42. PERFECT!
43. That's IT!
44. You're really improving.
45. Good work!
46. OUTSTANDING!
47. SENSATIONAL!
48. That's the best ever.
49. You must have been practicing.
50. You should be very proud of yourself.

Center for Effective Parenting (www.parents-ed.org)

Other websites recommended (www.cyberparent.com/esteem, www.jackcanfield.com/selfesteem.html, www.parents.com search for self-esteem, www.parents-talk.com)

La Fecha

Estimados Padres,

Un estudiante entra a la escuela como un individuo distintivo, formado por genes, medio ambiente, y cierto brillo dentro de sí mismo. Un incremento en la conciencia de cuan extraordinaria es la chispa que lo hace, ayuda al estudiante a preservar esa cualidad cuando la presión está en seguir a la multitud. Mi meta como consejero no es fabricar réplicas de los niños si no alimentar el espíritu individual de cada estudiante. Un viejo proverbio Chino dice, "Oigo y olvido, veo y recuerdo, y hago y comprendo."

Como niños todos nosotros requerimos aprender quien somos en el mundo. Y tal como aprendemos quienes somos, aprendemos a valuar y algunas veces a devaluar partes de nosotros mismos. Por ejemplo todos nosotros recibimos mensajes acerca de nuestros cuerpos, nuestras mentes, nuestros sentimientos y nuestras conductas. Debido a estos mensajes nosotros creamos conciencia de la autoestima. Quien somos en el mundo no es una información con la que nacemos. Es algo que adquirimos. Las experiencias que tenemos, y la respuesta de nuestras creencias que desarrollamos, establecen nuestro punto de vista de como encajamos en el mundo. Todos nosotros aprendimos esa lección de auto-evaluación (o devaluación) estando en relación con el mundo, sus elementos, y la gente que lo habita.

La autoestima puede ser definida como la manera en que la gente se percibe a si misma. Los niveles de autoestima de los niños son evidentes en su conducta y actitudes. Si los niños se sienten bien acerca de si mismos, estos buenos sentimientos serán reflejados en como se relacionan con amigos , maestros, hermanos, padres y otros. Autoestima es algo que afecta a los individuos durante toda su vida, por lo tanto, es muy importante que los padres ayuden a los niños a desarrollar niveles fuertes de autoestima. Hay muchas cosas que los padres pueden hacer para ayudar sus niños a aprender que ellos son amados, capaces, y competentes, empezando cuando ellos sean muy jóvenes. Desafortunadamente, también a edades muy tempranas los niños pueden empezar a desarrollar baja autoestima. Los padres deben de ser muy cuidadosos de no plantar en sus niños la semilla de la baja autoestima sin saberlo. Las siguientes normas ayudan a fomentar una positiva autoestima:

- ✓ No hacer comparasiones (ver cada niño como una contribución única aceptando al niño por lo que es y no por lo que uno quiere que sea).
- ✓ Expectativas Realistas (establezca metas para su hijo basado en quienes son y donde encajan en su desarrollo en la vida).
- ✓ Libertad para errores (no aliente perfeccionismo y ayude a los niños a resolver problemas que usan errores como experiencias).
- ✓ Oportunidades de éxito (cree situaciones para que los niños tengan éxito ayudandolos a resolver problemas por medio de cosas simples).
- ✓ Estímulo (premie a los niños por su esfuerzo en dar lo major en lugar de por ser los mejores; utilice discusión positiva y discuta su confianza).
- ✓ Acepte los sentimientos desagradables de los niños (todos los sentimientos son aceptados; hable acerca de ellos y discuta como están relacionados con la conducta de la persona).
- ✓ De opciones (esto genera propiedad y responsabilidad).
- ✓ De resposibilidad y espere cooperación (nunca haga por los niños lo que ellos puedan hacer por sí mismos).
- ✓ Mantenga el sentido del humor (estimule los niños a ver el lado amablede las cosas y a reirse de ellos mismos).

En el reverso de esta carta, he incluído "50 frases que los padres pueden decir para animar y premiar a sus hijos." Espero que encuentren útiles estas sugerencias del Centro de Ayuda para Padres.

Sinceramente,

Nombre

Titulo

Cincuenta Frases Que los Padres Pueden Decir a Sus Niños Para Premiarlos y Motivarlos

1. Estás en la dirección correcta!
2. Estás haciendo un buen trabajo!
3. Ya lo entendiste!
4. ESO ES CORRECTO!
5. Ya sabes como hacerlo!
6. Ese es el modo!
7. Ya lo tienes!
8. Bien hecho.
9. Lo hiciste ahora!
10. GRANDIOSO!
11. FANTASTICO!
12. TREMENDO!
13. TERRIFICO!
14. ¿Cómo lo hiciste?
15. Eso está mejor.
16. EXCELENTE!
17. Es la mejor cosa que has hecho.
18. Vas bien!
19. Eso está muy bien.
20. WAW!
21. Sigue con el buen trabajo.
22. Mucho mejor!
23. Bueno por tí!
24. SUPER!
25. Haces muy buen trabajo de _____.
26. Lo haces parecer muy fácil.
27. Muy bien.
28. Estás mejorando cada día.
29. MARAVILLOSO!
30. Sabía que podías hacerlo!
31. Lo estas haciendo maravillosamente.
32. Ese es el modo de hacerlo!
33. Sigue tratando.
34. Eres el mejor!
35. Lo estás haciendo mejor hoy.
36. Sigue trabajando en eso, lo estás haciendo mejor.
37. Eres muy bueno en eso.
38. Estoy muy orgulloso de tí.
39. Me gusta como escuchas.
40. Ya casi lo tienes.
41. Tú lo puedes hacer.
42. PERFECTO!
43. Eso es!
44. Realmente estás mejorando.
45. Buen trabajo!
46. SOBRESALIENTE!
47. SENSACIONAL!
48. Esta mejor que nunca.
49. Debes haber estado practicando.
50. Debes estar muy orgulloso de tí.

Centro para la Crianza Efectiva

Otras direcciones de internet recomendadas (busqueda de autoestima)

Bullying

"You can't always get what you want, BUT you can always be what you want."

—Keith Craft

(www.keithology.com)

Choose a book—

Hooway for Wodney Wat
or
The Brand New Kid

Make a poster to promote the book club.

Bullying Agenda

   I. Read one of the stories. (5 minutes)

  II. Group discussion questions. (10 minutes)

 III. My Personal Button activity. (10 minutes)

 IV. ABC's activity. (15 minutes)

  V. Go over bullying questionnaire. (if time permits)

 VI. Go over Telling Plan. (5 minutes)

Remind participants of next book club.

Send home parent letters.

Drawing for T-Shirt.

Intimidación

Hooway for Wodney Wat

Helen Lester

OBJETIVOS:

- ✓ Los participantes podrán definir diferentes tipos de intimidaciones.
- ✓ Los participantes conocerán los pasos a tomar si estan siendo intimidados.
- ✓ Los participantes identificarán cosas de las cuales los intimidadors toman ventaja.
- ✓ Los participantes entenderán como autoconvencimiento negativo les previene de acusar al intimidador y pedir ayuda.
- ✓ Los participantes discutirán la importancia de la confianza y lenguaje corporal tocante a los intimidadores.

Las preguntas para la Discusión del Grupo

(Está listo para discutir estas preguntas con todo detalle y la acción experimenta relacionado a ellos.)

1. ¿Cómo te tartan algunos niños cuando eres diferente? ¿Cuáles son algunos modos en que los intimidadores actúan hacía otros niños?
2. ¿Cómo el ser callado y tímido afecta la intimidación? ¿Por qué o por qué no? ¿Es una Buena idea estar solo cuando hay intimidadores cerca?
3. Camilla Capybara era una enorme intimidadora. ¿Son todos los intimidadores grandes?
4. ¿Qué usaba Camilla para tener poder sobre sus víctimas? ¿Qué pasa cuando el miedo te vence con los intimidadores?
5. ¿Cuáles son algunas maneras en que hayas visto niños siendo intimidados?
6. Wodney y los otros niños no le dijeron a nadie acerca de Camilla? ¿Crees que sea una Buena idea decirle a alguien en quien confías lo que está pasando? ¿Cómo te pueden ayudar?
7. ¿Qué pensamientos negativos te previenen de hablar con alguien acerca de el intimidador?
8. ¿Cómo la confianza y fuerte language corporal afecta al intimidador?
9. Deberías intimidar a otros? ¿Por qué crees que algunos niños intimidan a otros? ¿Puede alguien ser un intimidador sin proponerselo?
10. ¿Cuáles son algunas cosas que puedes hacer si eres intimidado?

Hooway for Wodney Wat

Helen Lester

OBJECTIVES:

- ✓ Participants will be able to define different types of bullying.
- ✓ Participants will know what steps to take if they are being bullied.
- ✓ Participants will identify different things that bullies take advantage of.
- ✓ Participants will understand how negative self talk will keep you from telling on a bully and getting help.
- ✓ Participants will discuss importance of confidence and body language in regards to bullies.

Questions for Group Discussion

(Be ready to discuss these questions in detail and share experiences related to them.)

1. How do some kids treat you when you are different? What are some of the ways bullies act toward other children?

2. How does being shy and quiet affect bullying? Why or Why not? Is being alone a good idea when bullies are around?

3. Camilla Capybara was a HUGE bully. Are all bullies big?

4. What did Camilla use to get power over her victims? What happens when you give in to fear with bullies?

5. What are some ways you've seen kids bullied?

6. Wodney and the other children didn't tell anyone about Camilla? Do you think it's a good idea to tell someone you trust about what is going on? How can they help you?

7. What negative thoughts keep you from talking to someone about a bully?

8. How does confidence and strong body language affect a bully?

9. Should you bully others? Why do you think kids bully others? Can someone be a bully without meaning to?

10. What are some things you can do if you are bullied?

Nino Nuevo

Katie Couric

Intimidación

OBJETIVOS:

- ✓ Los participantes definirán la intimidación.
- ✓ Los participantes discutirán diferentes cosas de las cuales los intimidadores se aprovechan.
- ✓ Los participantes discutirán originalidad.
- ✓ Los participantes discutirán opciones de acuerdo a conducta intimidante.
- ✓ Los participantes dicutirán como hace sentir a la gente la intimidación.
- ✓ Los participantes encontrarán modos de combatir la intimidación.

Las preguntas para la Discusión del Grupo

(Está listo para discutir estas preguntas con todo detalle y la acción experimenta relacionado a ellos.)

1. El primer día de escuela siempre es un poquito intimidador. ¿Cómo fue peor aún para Lazlo?

2. ¿Cómo llamarías a cómo lo estaban tratando los niños? ¿Cómo crees que Lazlo se sintió?

3. ¿Por qué los otros niños fueron malos con Lazlo? Pareció como si todos lo "atacaran." ¿Es fácil ser malo o irrespetuoso con alguien cuando estás en grupo?

4. ¿Ser "diferente" es algo malo? ¿Por qué o por qué no? ¿Cuáles son algunas cosas que son diferentes acerca de tí?

5. Los niños molestaban a Lazlo por muchas rezones diferentes. Cuáles son algunas de las cosas por las cuales los intimidadores podrían "molestar" a la gente? La mama de Lazlo estaba muy molesta. ¿Crees que la intimidación afecta a toda la familia? ¿Por qué o por qué no?

6. ¿Qué significa "buscar lo bueno de las personas?" ¿Crees que esa es una elección que todos podemos hacer? ¿Crees que todos tienen algo bueno en su interior?

7. La señorita Kincaid no era de mucha ayuda con los intimidadores. Básicmente ella los ignoraba y trataba de distraerlos. ¿Comó crees que los adultos pueden ayudar en situaciones de intimidación?

8. Lazlo fue el ultimo es ser escogido para softbol. ¿Aguna ves tú has sido el ultimo en ser escogido? ¿Cómo te sentiste? ¿Significa eso que no eres una buena persona?

9. ¿Cuáles son algunos modos en que podemos ayudar si vemos a alguien que está siendo intimidado o fastidiado?

10. ¿Qué hizo Ellie para hacer la diferencia? ¿Por qué fue eso importante?

11. ¿Puede una persona hacer la diferencia? ¿Por qué o por qué no? ¿Es importante decirle a alguien que estás siendo intimidado? ¿Cuáles son algunas razones por las cuales algunos niños prefiere no decirlo?

Available in Spanish

The Brand New Kid

Katie Couric

OBJECTIVES:

- ✓ Participants will define bulling.
- ✓ Participants will discuss different things that bullies pick on.
- ✓ Participants will discuss uniqueness.
- ✓ Participants will discuss choices regarding bullying behavior.
- ✓ Participants will discuss how bullying makes people feel.
- ✓ Participants will find ways to combat bullying.

Questions for Group Discussion

(Be ready to discuss these questions in detail and share experiences related to them.)

1. The first day of school is always a little scary. How was it even worse for Lazlo? What do you call how the children were treating him? How do you think Lazlo felt?

2. Why were the other children mean to Lazlo? It seemed like everyone "ganged up" on him. Is it easier to be mean or disrespectful to someone when you're in a group?

3. Is being "different" a bad thing? Why or why not? What are some things that are different about you?

4. The children picked on Lazlo for many different reasons. What are some things that bullies might "bug" people about? Lazlo's mom was very upset. Do you think bullying affects the whole family? Why or why not?

5. What does it mean "To look for the good in people?" Do you think that's a choice we can all make? Do you think everyone has something good inside them?

6. Miss Kincaid wasn't much help with the bullies. She basically ignored them and tried to distract them. How do you think adults can help in bullying situations?

7. Lazlo was the last one picked for softball. Have you ever been the last one picked? How did that make you feel? Does that mean you're not a good person?

8. What are some ways we can help if we see someone being bullied or teased?

9. What did Ellie do to make a difference? Why was that important?

10. Can one person make a difference? Why or why not? Is it important to tell someone about being bullied? What are some reasons kids might not tell?

The Telling Plan

Who:
- ❖ friends
- ❖ parents
- ❖ teacher
- ❖ phone line
- ❖ counselor, trusted adult...

When:
- ❖ after school
- ❖ when you have an adult alone
- ❖ during private time

What:
- ❖ how often the bullying is happening
- ❖ who is involved
- ❖ what do they do
- ❖ how does it make you feel...

How to Tell:
- ❖ writing a letter or email
- ❖ take a friend with you
- ❖ drawing
- ❖ poem
- ❖ ask someone to tell for you
  (REMEMBER IT IS BEST FOR YOU TO HAVE COURAGE AND ACTUALLY BE INVOLVED IN THE STRATEGY)...

If you don't tell, things won't get better! Results of not taking care of bullies are serious and affect children in big ways. Below are some of the results of not telling:
- ❑ Bullying continues
- ❑ Children begin to feel sick and afraid
- ❑ Children can't concentrate
- ❑ Children don't want to go back to school
- ❑ Bullying moves to new victim (even if the bully decides to leave you alone, he/she will move onto the next victim...maybe one of your friends

My Personal Button

Objective: Create awareness of the role that each individual plays in alleviating bullying situations.

Materials: Button maker or cut circles (from cardboard or posterboard), safety pins, glue, decorative items, laminater

Procedure: Tell students that they are going to design buttons with slogans and pictures representing a "No Bullying Allowed" campus. Explain that each student is to create a button that they will wear discouraging bullying at school. Buttons can have a picture, decorations, slogan, anything that encourages taking a stand against bullies. After students create their buttons, help them to glue a safety with a glue gun to the back of the button. (This could also be done with stickers if you had a sticker maker). After the buttons are complete have students share with the group what their button means and how they feel about bullying.

You could even take this to a whole other level with having students create and organize a "No Bullying Day" complete with slogans, buttons, activities, rules, and so forth.

The ABC's of *not* Being a Bully

Objective: Understanding of bullying behaviors as well as coping strategies.

Materials: White paper, crayons, markers, drawing materials, spiral binders and binding machine

Procedure: After disussing bullying with children in detail as well as strategies, tell students that they are going to make an ABC Book of how not to bully that will be displayed in the library (you could also do this in the computer lab if you wanted to utilize technology). Assign students letters of the alphabet and have them come up with something that correlates that letter of the alphabet with a bullying topic. For example, "A" might stand for acceptance of everyone, "B" belonging helps others feel good. To get students thinking say, "Sometimes it is difficult to know what is or is not bullying. Often, actions start out just being fun, but may at some point actually turn into bullying. If you are not sure whether something has become bullying, stop and think and ask yourself these questions:

1. Are my actions or words hurting someone else's feelings?
2. Are my actions or words hurting someone else physically or making that person feel afraid?
3. Would I want someone else to do this to me?
4. Am I unfairly taking my anger out on someone?
5. Am I trying to control someone against his or her will?

After students complete all letters and they put them together, help them to use the binding machine to spiral bind their book together for display in the library.

DeDe Coffman

Right it Up

Objective: Create awareness of bullying and the feelings associated with the victim and bully.

Materials: Paper or computer, paints, butcher paper.

Procedure: After discussing bullying completing, put students into two different groups. Have one group of students write a poem from the perspective of a bully. Use lots of adjectives and really discuss how the bully feels and behaves. The other group needs to write a poem from the victims perspective. Include feelings, emotions, and possible strategies for overcoming the bullying. When students complete poems, have someone read each poem outloud for a discussion.

After poems have been read, allow students one at a time to come up and paint a portion of a bullying scene on the mural. Each student will add to what the previous student has done. (No one will really know how the mural will turn out until the end.) The goal is for the picture to show a positive encounter with a bully. Each student has a set amount of time to paint.

Bullying Survey

Directions: Please circle or underline the best answers to the following questions. You may have more than one best answer for some questions. You do not have to put your name on the paper.

Name (optional)_____

1. Have you ever been bullied?

   yes   or   no

   If you answered yes, how often did someone bully you?
   Occasionally   Often   Every day

   Where did it happen?
   School   Park   Home   Neighborhood   Somewhere else

   If it happened at school, where?
   Hallway   Classroom   Playground   Cafeteria   Bathroom   Somewhere else

2. Have you witnessed bullied at school?

   yes   or   no

   If you answered yes, how often did it happen?
   Occasionally   Often   Every day

   Where have you seen other students bullied?
   Hallway   Classroom   Playground   Cafeteria   Bathroom   Somewhere else

3. What kinds of things have bullies done to you or to someone you know?
   teasing threatening stealing or damaged something physical hitting ignored

4. How much of a problem is bullying for you?
   Very much   Not much   None

5. What are some things you think parents, teachers, and other adults could do to stop bullying?

DeDe Coffman

Date

Dear Parents,

Bullying hurts. It makes people miserable. It can change lives forever. The bullying problem can only be solved if young people and adults act together. Finding out that your child is being bullied is a stressful and distressing experience. It's natural for a parent to feel anger, confusion and guilt. Some children are good at hiding their feelings and the first you may know of the problem is when your child suddenly doesn't want to go to school, or says they are ill when PE lessons are on the agenda. Other pointers can be:

- Coming home with cuts and bruises
- Torn clothes
- Asking for stolen possessions to be replaced
- 'Losing' dinner money
- Falling out with previously good friends
- Being moody and bad tempered
- Being quiet and withdrawn
- Wanting to avoid leaving the house
- Aggression with brothers and sisters
- Doing less well at schoolwork
- Insomnia
- Anxiety

The worst thing to do is to over-react and storm into school demanding action. If you think your young child is being bullied, but you're not sure, then ask a few simple questions:

- What did they do at school today?
- Did they do anything they liked?
- Did they do anything they didn't like?
- Who did they play with?
- What sort of games did they play?
- Did they enjoy them?
- Would they have liked to play different games with someone else?
- Are they looking forward to going to school tomorrow?

The number one concern of parents across the United States according to new polls is if their child is safe at schools. Bullying comprises a big part of those worries. If we all work together, we can teach bullies different ways of behaving and at the same time empower their victims to be confident and stand up for themselves. I have included on the back of this letter some quotes from different people involved in a bullying situation. I found them interesting. If you have any questions, please feel free to call me at school.

Sincerely,

Name

Title

Some quotations about bullying...

Victim: "When I was at primary school I got picked on non-stop for two years. No-one talked to me. I hadn't done anything to get blamed for, and I still don't know the reason I got picked on. I wasn't any wealthier or poorer or a different race. I used to cry myself to sleep every night. I was miserable. My parents knew and they talked to the headmaster but he wasn't interested and said he couldn't do anything about it. My parents knew all the bullies' parents. One girl even lived in the same street and we had been friends since we were two. Like a sheep she dumped me because no-one else talked to me.

This all happened in primary 6 and I have lost nearly all my self-confidence and hate being on my own. I'd hate to think this was happening to anyone else. I have a fear that if one girl doesn't talk to me they will all start again and it will never stop. I don't want it to go on for the rest of my school life. I couldn't cope." (girl, 14)

Bully: "I have never actually set out to bully someone myself. It usually comes about when someone is being annoyed and provides an amusing reaction that I begin to join in. At the time you do not see it as bullying, although you may have doubts later. I do not think there is anyone at school who has not bullied someone in one way or another." (boy, 16)

Parent: "My daughter has been bullied since she was at primary school. Daily she is called names like 'b——' and 'slag'. We have tried everything but no-one listens. She has threatened to kill herself. All she wants is to be a happy kid at school with friends. I don't want any parent to suffer what we have suffered. I shall continue to fight."

School: "People could either say, 'That's a terrible school because they have bullying', or they could say, 'That's a good school because they are facing up to it,' - we decided to take the risk." (Headteacher whose school decided to launch an anti-bullying program)

Websites worth looking at that discuss bullying:

http://www.scre.ac.uk/bully/

http://www.antibullying.net/

http://www.bullying.co.uk/

La Fecha

Estimados Padres,

La intimidación lastima. Hace a la gente miserable. Puede cambiar vidas para siempre. El problema de la intimidación puede ser resuelto solamente si los jóvenes y los adultos actúan juntos. Descubrir que su hijo está siendo intimidado es una experiencia penosa y estresante. Es natural para muchos padres sentir enojo, confusión y culpa. Algunos niños son buenos ocultando sus sentimientos y la primer señal del problema es cuando el niño repentinamente no quiere ir a la escuela, o dice que está enfermo cuando le toca Educación Física. Otros puntos pueden ser:

- Llegar a la casa con moretones y cortadas
- Ropa desgarrada
- Pedir que se le repongan cosas robadas
- 'Perder' el dinero de la comida
- Perder buenos amigos anteriores
- Estar irritable y de mal temperamento
- Estar muy serio y aislado
- Evitar salir de la casa
- Agresión con hermanos y hermanas
- Salir mal en su escuela
- Insomnia
- Ansiedad

La peor cosa por hacer es exagerar e ir a la escuela demandando acción. Si usted piensa que su pequeño hijo está siendo intimidado, pero no está seguro, entonces haga unas simples preguntas:

- ¿Qué hicieron en la escuela hoy?
- ¿Hicieron algo que les gustó?
- ¿Hicieron algo que no les gustó?
- ¿Con quién jugaron?
- ¿Qué clase de juegos jugaron?
- ¿Los disfrutaron?
- ¿Les hubiera gustado jugar otros juegos con otras personas?
- ¿Están interesados en ir a la escuela mañana?

La preocupación número uno de los padres en los Estados Unidos según las recientes encuestas es si sus niños están seguros en las escuelas. Intimidación comprende una gran parte de sus preocupaciones. Si todos trabajamos juntos, podemos enseñar a los intimidadores diferentes conductas y al mismo tiempo darle poder a sus víctimas a tener más confianza y defenderse por ellos mismos. He incluído al reverso de esta carta algunas frases de diferentes personas involucradas en situaciones de intimidación. Me parecieron interesantes. Si tiene algúna pregunta, por favor con toda confianza llámeme a la escuela.

Sinceramente,

Nombre

Titulo

Víctima: "Cuándo estaba en la primaria fui molestado constantemente durante dos años. Nadie me hablaba. No había hecho nada para que me culparan, y aún no sé la razón por la cuál me molestaban. No era más rico o más pobre o de una raza diferente. Cada noche lloraba hasta dormirme. Era miserable. Mis padres supieron y hablaron con el director de la escuela pero él no estaba interesado y dijo que no podía hacer nada acerca de eso. Mis padres conocían a los padres de todos los intimidadores. Inclusive una niña vivía en la misma calle y habíamos sido amigos desde que teníamos dos años. Como una borrega ella también dejo de hablarme como todos los demás.

Todo esto pasó en sexto año de primaria y desde entonces casi he perdido la confianza en mi mismo y odio estar sólo. Odiaba pensar que le estuviera pasando a alguien más. Tengo miedo de que si alguna muchacha no me habla todos ellos empezaran otra vez y nunca se detendrá. No quiero que suceda por el resto de mi vida escolar. No podría soportarlo." (muchacha, 14)

Intimidador: "Nunca me he propuesto intimidar a nadie. Usualmente sucede cuando alguien se está molestando y provee una reacción divertida que empiezo a tomar parte de eso. En ese momento no ves que es intimidación, aunque puedes tener dudas más tarde. No creo que haya alguien en la escuela que de una manera o de otra no haya intimidado a alguien." (muchacho, 16)

Padre: "Mi hija ha sido intimidada desde que estaba en la primaria. Diariamente le dicen nombres como 'b——' y 'escoria'. Hemos tratado de todo pero nadie escucha. Ella ha amenazado con matarse. Todo lo que ella quiere es ser una niña feliz con sus amigos en la escuela. No quiero que ningún padre sufra lo que hemos sufrido. Continuaré luchando."

Escuela: "La gente podría decir, 'Es una escuela terrible porque tienen intimidación ', o pudieran decir, 'Es una Buena escuela porque lo están encarando,' – decidimos tomar el riezgo." (Maestra cuya escuela decidio lanzar un programa de anti-intimidación)

Direcciones electronicas en intimidación que vale la pena ver:

http://www.scre.ac.uk/bully/

http://www.antibullying.net/

http://www.bullying.co.uk/

Girls and Bullying

"To the world
you're one person,
but to one person,
you may be the
world."

—unknown

Choose a book—

The English Roses
or
The Recess Queen

Make a poster to promote the book club.

Girls and Bullying Agenda

  I. Read one of the stories. (5 minutes)

 II. Group Discussion questions. (10 minutes)

III. Mirror, Mirror. (10 minutes)

IV. What's Cooking? (15 minutes)

Remind kids about next book club

Send home parent letters

Draw for T-Shirt

muchachas y conducta

Las Rosas Inglesas

MaDonna

OBJETIVOS:

- ✓ Los participantes definiran intimidación tocante a muchachas
- ✓ Los participantes analizarán como los grupos afectan la conducta
- ✓ Los participantes discutirán encelamiento
- ✓ Los participantes discutirán juzgando a otros

Las preguntas para la Discusión del Grupo

(Está listo para discutir estas preguntas con todo detalle y la acción experimenta relacionado a ellos.)

1. ¿Crees que hay tendencia a haber problemas cuando grupos de muchachas se juntan como las Rosas Inglesas? ¿Por qué? ¿Qué pasa con frecuencia? ¿Cómo tratan a la gente? ¿Su conducta se llamaría intimidación? ¿Por qué o por qué no?

2. ¿Cuál es el lado positivo y negativo de pertenecer a un club o grupo? ¿Puede alguien ser un intimidador sin proponerselo? ¿Cómo?

3. ¿Qué es encelamiento? El encelamiento realmente parece ser un problema de las Rosas Inglesas. ¿Por qué crees que era eso? ¿Crees que encelamiento es una de las grandes rezones por las cuales las muchachas son malas entre sí? ¿Qué crees que se pueda hacer acerca de esto?

4. Además de encelamiento, ¿cuáles son otras cosas que hacen que las muchachas se traten una a otra irrespetuosamente?

5. Las Rosas Inglesas excluyeron, aislaron, y se le quedaron viendo a Binah. ¿Cuáles son otras maneras en que las muchachas intimidan? ¿Cuál lastima más?

6. Binah estaba muy sola. ¿Alguna vez te has sentido solo? ¿Qué te hizo sentir mejor? ¿Crees que puedes hacer la diferencia cuándo ves a alguien que está solo?

7. ¿Por qué para nosotros es tan díficil ayudar a alguien cuando vemos que está siendo intimidado?

8. La vida de Binah no era lo que las Rosas Inglesas creían. ¿Crees que algunas veces nosotros juzgamos mal a otros? ¿Cómo podemos evitar eso?

Available in Spanish

girls and behavior

The English Roses

MaDonna

OBJECTIVES:

- ✓ Participants will define bullying as it pertains to girls
- ✓ Participants will analyze how groups affect behavior
- ✓ Participants will discuss jealousy
- ✓ Participants will discuss judging others

Questions for Group Discussion

(Be ready to discuss these questions in detail and share experiences related to them.)

1. Do you think there tends to be a problem when groups of girls get together like the English Roses? Why? What often happens? How do they treat people? Would call their behavior bullying? Why or Why not?

2. What is the positive and negative side of belonging to a club or group? Can someone be a bully without meaning to? How?

3. What is jealousy? Jealousy seem to really be an issue for the English Roses. Why do you think that was? Do you think jealousy is one of the big reasons why girls act mean toward one another? What do you think can be done about this?

4. Besides jealousy, what are some other things that make girls treat each other disrespectful?

5. The English Roses excluded, isolated, and stared at Binah. What are some other ways that girls bully? Which one hurts the worst?

6. Binah was very lonely. Have you ever felt lonely? What made you feel better? Do you think that you can make a difference when you see someone who is lonely?

7. Why is hard for us to stand up for someone when we see bullying happening?

8. Binah's life was not at all what the English Roses thought. Do you think we misjudge others sometimes? How can we not do that?

girls and bullying

The Recess Queen

Alexis O'Neill

OBJETIVOS:

- ✓ Los participantes definirán como intimidan las muchachas
- ✓ Los participantes entenderán la hechura de un intimidador
- ✓ Los participantes discutirán estrategias para lidear con un intimidador

Las preguntas para la Discusión del Grupo

(Está listo para discutir estas preguntas con todo detalle y la acción experimenta relacionado a ellos.)

1. ¿Qué es intimidación? ¿Intimidan las muchachas diferente que los muchachos? ¿Cómo?

2. ¿Has visto alguna vez intimidación en el parque? Discute.

3. ¿Qué crees que hace a un intimidador actuar agresivo hacia otros? Discute.

4. Hay una Mean Jean en tú vida? ¿Cómo actúa?

5. Mean Jean se sintió poderosa en el cuento. ¿Crees que a los intimidadores les gusta sentirse poderosos? ¿Qué puedes hacer para quitarles su poder?

6. ¿Qué es valor? ¿Se necesita valor para enfrentarse a un intimidador? ¿Qué evita que la gente se defienda o defienda a otros?

7. ¿Cuáles son algunas maneras de protejerte de intimidadores?

8. ¿Cuál es la diferencia entre intimidación y bromear?

girls and bullying

The Recess Queen

Alexis O'Neill

OBJECTIVES:

✓ Participants will define how girls bully
✓ Participants will understand the makeup of a bully
✓ Participants will discuss strategies for dealing with a bully

Questions for Group Discussion

(Be ready to discuss these questions in detail and share experiences related to them.)

1. What is bullying? Do girls bully differently than boys? How?
2. Have you ever seen bullying happening on the playground? Discuss.
3. What do you think makes a bully act aggressive toward others? Discuss.
4. Is there a Mean Jean in your life? How does she act?
5. Mean Jean felt powerful in the story. Do you think bullies like to feel powerful? What can you do to take away their power?
6. What is courage? Does it take courage to stand up to a bully? What keeps people from standing up for themselves or others?
7. How are some ways that you can protect yourself from bullies?
8. What's the difference between bullying and fooling around?

Mirror Mirror

Objectives: Reflect on what is really important as a girl in comparison with what the world shows us is important; create awareness of behavior

Materials: Mirrors (double-sided), drawing paper, markers, crayons, glue, magazines

Procedures: Discuss how the media and the world sometimes portrays the "perfect girl." Ask participants what is really most important in being a girl. Pass out a mirror to each girl. Have them look at theirselves in the mirror and reflect silently which image discussed above they most want to be. Have girls create two drawings or pictures reflecting the differences discussed above. After completing drawings, place them on the mirrors for the girls to take home. Tell girls to check themselves each morning to see what type of girl they are going to try to be each day. At night, they can re-check to see if they were successful. (This is a great way to get girls thinking about their behavior and creating awareness of behavior). You could also use magazines for cutting and pasting if you didn't want to have them draw; however, it might be hard to find a picture of what's really important as a girl. You could let them use the magazine for the world's vision of the "perfect girl" and then draw what's really important.

After mirror activities are completed, have participants draw for bullying scenarios to role play. Situations might included the following:

- making fun of how someone looks
- "accidentally" bumping into someone in the hall
- calling names or teasing because of clothes, skin color, and so forth.
- making kids play games your way
- telling someone that what they are wearing doesn't look good on them
- group of kids not letting someone sit with them at lunch when there is plenty of room
- joking with people by putting them down or isolating them
- ANTI BULLYING telling someone they aren't being nice!

What's Cooking?

Objective: Disuss ways to help with the unhappiness felt by bullying; learn strategies for overcoming a bullying situation.

Materials: Unhappiness worksheets, recipe cards, markers, baked item (optional), an example of a recipe

Procedure: Ask participants how do you change unhappiness into happiness. Tell them you don't have to be a magician. You only have to use your head. Create together an acrostic with the word UNHAPPINESS to spell out things you could do to turn unhappiness into happiness. (allow students to make their unique or go along with the group). An example to use with students might be that the "U" could stand for "understanding" because with a bully it's important to understand what's behind the bullying....

After students create the acrostics, put students in groups and have them create a recipe for how to handle a bully so that they can prevent the unhappiness that comes along with it. For example, ingredients might include some of the strategies from the acrostic. This could be done in the computer lab to utilize technology. It might be fun as well to bring something you've made for the children to eat to discuss how recipes are made up. Children always love to eat!

UNHAPPINESS

Recipe for: _____

From the Kitchen of: _____

Ingredients: _____

_____

_____

_____

_____

Directions: _____

_____

_____

_____

Date

Dear Parents,

Look at the beautiful girl with the honey-blond hair. She always has plenty of admiring friends and clothes to die for. She has everything, but popularity isn't always what it seems. She and other adolescent girls live in a world where best friends can become adversaries overnight, where one look from another girl can mean the difference between loneliness and fitting in. It's a world where no one tells you why you can no longer sit at the lunch table with your friends, where secrets like trading cards.

Adolescent and preadolescent girls exercise mammoth influence over their peers. Their arsenal — gossiping, name-calling, excluding—may not give other girls black eyes or bloody lips, but they can be as destructive as physical bullying, brutality, and racial slurs. These frequently secret acts of aggression also affect your school climate and culture, as well as the girls' grades and sense of self-worth.

Bullying doesn't just happen with girls, but girls tend to use relationships to bully more than boys. We know this: kids are hurting. And hurting kids that aren't repaired turn into adults unable to cope with life. American society increasingly ignores that violence has become acceptable behavior. Though we've taken great measure to remove weapons and calm raging fists, we still allow emotional violence to occur without consequence. Violence occurs on a continuum. Something as seemingly harmless as eye-rolling on one end to suicide and school shootings on the other low end of the continuum. By targeting relational aggression (gossip, rumor-spreading, exclusion), we can prevent hurtful behavior inflicting major psychological damage on ALL people.

We must as a "village" take this type of bullying seriously. I read an awesome article out of the Amercian School Board Journal that I think everyone adult needs to read. You can locate the article online at http://www.asbj.com/2002/08/0802coverstory.html. I encourage you to take a look at it! As always I'm here to help. Let me know if you want more information on this hot topic. Thanks for all you do to support our children!

Sincerely,

Name
Title

La Fecha

Estimados Padres,

Mira a la Hermosa muchacha con pelo de miel. Siempre tiene suficientes admiradores y ropa para morir. Ella lo tiene todo, pero la popularidad no es siempre lo que parece. Ella y otras muchachas adolecentes viven en un mundo donde las mejores amigas se pueden convertir en enemigas de la noche a la mañana, cuando la aparencia física de otra muchacha puede significar la diferencia entre la soledad y el encajar. Es un mundo donde nadie te dice porque ya no te puedes sentar en la cafetería con tus amigas, donde los secretos son como tarjetas de intercambio.

Muchachas preadolescents y adolescents ejercen una enorme influencia sobre sus compañeras. Su arsenal—chismes, apodos, exclusión – pueden no ponerle un ojo morado a otras muchachas o labios ensangrentados, pero puede ser tan destructivo como intimidación física, brutalidad, y menosprecio racial. Estos actos de agresión frecuentemente secretos afectan además el ambiente y cultura de tu escuela, también como las calificaciones de las muchachas y el sentido de autoestima.

Intimidación no sucede solo con las muchachas, pero las muchachas tienen la tendencia de usar relaciones para intimidar más que los muchachos. Sabemos esto: **Los ninos se están lastimando.** Y los niños lastimados que no se reparan se convierten en adultos incapaces de hacerle frente a la vida. La sociedad americana crecientemente ignora que la violencia se ha transformado en conducta aceptable. Aún cuando hemos tomado grandes medidas para remover armas y calmar los puños, aún permitimos que la violencia emocional ocurra sin consecuencias. La violencia ocurre continuamente. Desde algo que parece tan inofensivo como un gesto de los ojos por un lado hasta el suicidio y las balaceras por el otro. Atacando agresiones relativas (rumores, diseminando-rumores, exclusión), podemos prevenir conductas perjudiciales que infligen daño psicológico mayor en TODA la gente.

Debemos como una "villa" tomar este tipo de intimidación seriamente. Leí un imponente artículo en el Amercian School Board Journal que creo que todo adulto necesita leer. Puede localizar el artículo en el internet en la dirección . Lo anímo a que lo vea! Como siempre estoy aquí para ayudar. Digame si quiere más información en este tema. ¡Gracias por todo lo que hace para apoyar a nuestros niños!

Sinceramente,

Nombre

Titulo

Prejudice

"Books are the carriers of civilization. Without books, history is silent, literature dumb, science crippled, thought and speculations at a standstill."

—Barbara Tuchman

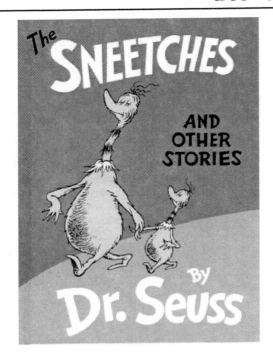

Choose a book—

The Sneetches
or
Rainbow Fish to the Rescue

Make a poster to promote the book club.

DeDe Coffman

Prejudice Agenda

  I. Read one of the stories together. (5 minutes)

 II. Group discussion questions. (10 minutes)

III. A Bit of An Apple activity. (10 minutes)

IV. Worthiness activity. (10 minutes)

 V. Prejudice Pledge. (5 minutes)

Remind about next book club

Send home parent letters

Drawing for t-shirt

(You could also incorporate the video of the Sneetches into this book club session.)

The Sneetches

Dr. Seuss

OBJETIVOS:

- ✓ Los participantes celebrarán diferencias individuales.
- ✓ Los participantes identificarán estereotipia.
- ✓ Los participantes discutirán diferentes modos en que gente prejuiciosa trata a otros.
- ✓ Los participantes entenderán que significa respeto para toda la gente.

Las preguntas para la Discusión del Grupo

(Está listo para discutir estas preguntas con todo detalle y la acción experimenta relacionado a ellos.)

1. ¿Cuales fueron algunas de las maneras en que los Sneetches mostraron prejuicio en el cuento?

2. ¿Alguna vez has presenciado o tomado parte en una de estos tipos de conducta? ¿Cómo crees que los "Plain Bellied Sneetches" se sintieron? El Dr. Seuss dice que "Los dejaron afuera en el frío y la oscuridad de las playas." ¿Cómo se siente que lo dejen a uno afuera en la oscuridad? ¿Es importante que no hagamos sentir a la gente de ese modo?

3. ¿Qué hizo diferente a los Sneetches en el cuento? ¿Cuáles son algunas de las cosas que en la vida real dividen a la gente?

4. ¿Qué es estereotipia? ¿Cómo está esto relacionado con prejuicio?

5. Una de las estrategias que los "Plain Bellied Sneetches" usaron para sobreponerse al prejuicio y estereotipia fue cambiar su apariencia añadiendo estrellas a sus vientres. ¿Ayuda siempre cambiar quien eres para ser aceptado? ¿Por qué o por qué no?

6. ¿Por qué crees que es tratada mal la gente que es diferente?

7. ¿Cuáles son algunas de las cosas que podemos hacer para asegurar igualdad y respeto para todos?

8. En el final del cuento, ¿cómo resuelven su problema los Sneetches? ¿Crees que la respuesta es aceptación? ¿Por qué o por qué no? ¿Necesitas a alguien como McMonkey McBean para resolver los problemas de prejuicio o es algo que podemos hacer juntos?

The Sneetches

Dr. Seuss

OBJECTIVES:

- ✓ Participants will celebrate differences in individuals.
- ✓ Participants will identify stereotyping.
- ✓ Participants will discuss different ways prejudice people treat others.
- ✓ Participants will understand what respect for all people means.

Questions for Group Discussion

(Be ready to discuss these questions in detail and share experiences related to them.)

1. What were some of the ways that the Sneetches showed prejudice in the story? Have you ever witnessed or been a part of any of these types of behavior? How do you think the "Plain Bellied Sneetches" felt?

2. Dr. Seuss says that "They left them out cold in the dark of the beaches." How does it feel to be left out in the dark? Is it important that we don't make people feel this way?

3. What made the Sneetches different in the story? What are some of the things you know about that divide people in real life?

4. What is stereotyping? How is this related to prejudice?

5. One of the strategies the "Plain Bellied Sneetches" used to overcome the prejudice and stereotyping was to change how they looked by adding stars to their bellies. Does it ever help to change who you are to fit in? Why or why not?

6. Why do you think people who are different are treated badly?

7. What are some things we can do to ensure equality and respect for all?

8. In the end of the story, how did the Sneetches solve their problem? Do you think acceptance is the answer? Why or why not? Do you need anyone like McMonkey McBean to solve the problems of prejudice or is it something that we can all do together?

Pez Arco Iris Al Rescate

Marcus Pfister

OBJETIVOS:

- ✓ Los participantes discutirán persepciones é ideas preconcevidas.
- ✓ Los participantes discutirán similaridades y diferencias en la gente.
- ✓ Los participantes definirán prejuicio.
- ✓ Los participantes entenderán los efectos negativos de prejuicio y estereotipia en individuos y sociedades.

Las preguntas para la Discusión del Grupo

(Está listo para discutir estas preguntas con todo detalle y la acción experimenta relacionado a ellos.)

1. ¿Qué es prejuicio? Rainbow Fish habla de no ser solo un pez ordinario—¿Cómo crees que siendo ordinario y normal está relacionado en como la gente se trata una a la otra?

2. Los pescados en el cuento han jugado juntos siempre. Se han convertido en un grupo muy unido? ¿Cuál es el lado positivo de esto? ¿Cuál es el lado negativo de esto?

3. ¿Cuándo el pescado rayado paso nadando, el otro pescado se le quedó mirando. ¿Alguna vez se te han quedado viendo? ¿Cómo te sentiste? ¿Crees que la gente que es diferente y que vemos fijamente se siente igual?

4. ¿Qué es exclusión? ¿Es una forma de prejuicio? ¿Alguna vez has sido excluído?

5. ¿Has estado alguna vez en un grupo donde hubo exclusión y no sabías que hacer? ¿Qué te previno de alcanzar a la persona que estaba siendo excluída? Recapacitando, que hubieras podido hacer?

6. Qué tan importante es como te ves? ¿Por qué? ¿Como te ves por fuera tiene algo que ver con lo que puede haber dentro?

7. Un tiburón trajo peligro al cuento del Pescado Arcoiris. ¿Cómo es peligroso el prejuicio? ¿Qué se pierde cuando la gente no es aceptada por lo que son?

8. ¿Cuáles son algunas maneras de combatir la estereotipia y el prejuicio? ¿Es aterrador oponerte a algo malo? ¿Por qué? ¿Puedes hacer la diferencia?

Available in Spanish

Rainbow Fish to the Rescue
Marcus Pfister

OBJECTIVES:

- ✓ Participants will discuss perceptions and preconceived ideas.
- ✓ Participants will discuss similarities and differences in people.
- ✓ Participants will define prejudice.
- ✓ Participants will understand the negative effects of prejudice and stereotyping on individuals and societies.

Questions for Group Discussion

(Be ready to discuss these questions in detail and share experiences related to them.)

1. What is prejudice? Rainbow Fish talks about not being just ordinary fish—How do you think being ordinary and normal is related to how people treat each other?

2. The fish in the story had played together forever. They had become a close group. Is it a good thing for people to always be togther? What is the positive side to this? What is the negative side to this?

3. When the striped fish swam through, the other fish stared at him. Have you ever been stared at? How did it make you feel? Do you think people we stare at because they are different feel the same way?

4. What is exclusion? Is it a form of prejudice? Have you ever been excluded?

5. Have you ever been in a group where exclusion was taking place but you didn't know what to do? What kept you from reaching out to the excluded person? Looking back, what could you have done?

6. How important is the way you look? Why? Does how you look on the outside have anything to do with what might be on the inside?

7. A shark brought danger into the Rainbow Fish story. How is prejudice dangerous? What is lost when people are not accepted for who they are?

8. What are some ways we can fight stereotyping and prejudice? Is it scary to take a stand against something bad? Why? Can you make a difference?

A Bit of An Apple

Objective: Show children that all people make look different, but what's on the inside is what's important; explain to children about potential and that we shouldn't judge people by outward appearance; engage children in learning about inner strength and goodness.

Materials: Apples of different shapes, sizes, and colors; a knife

Procedures: Show children several apples discussing differences about how the apples look on the outside (size, color, bruising, shriveled, and so forth). Cut apples in half (not lengthwise) but across the apple. Begin discussing with students the seed pod. Talk about how all apples have a similar five-star inside that holds seeds. Ask students is the outside condition of the apples have any effect on the seeds inside.

Ask how humans are like the apples. Lead students in a discussion about the outward appearances of people (size, shapes, colors, ages, and so forth). Explain to students that inside all people are the same seeds of worth and greatness as the apple. People have similar stars inside them that shine and hel them grow and become a person with something to offer the world. Just like an apple tree, if people are properly nourished, accepted, and loved, extraordinary things can happen in their lives. Discuss how we shouldn't judge people by outward appearances. Qualities like size, shape, color, beauty, age, family, houses, religions, and so forth. aren't important. What's important is inner strength and greatness.

Ask children if they know anyone who is not very pretty or handsome, but who is very nice? Talk about heroes and why they are heroes. Discuss heroes fully and compare insides with outsides of these people. Ask what it takes to make an apple tree grow and compare that with what it takes to help people become great. Also, ask if they can think of a time when they judged someone without knowing them.

After discussion and demonstrations, allow students to eat apples.

DeDe Coffman

Worthiness

Objective: Show similarities and differences between two objects that have the same worth and value.

Materials: A dollar bill and 100 pennies

Procedures: Hold up the dollar bill and the pennies. Ask everyone to look them over and try to determine all the ways the bill and coins differ. Discuss this thoroughly (hardness of pennies versus softness and flexibility of dollar bill; pennies make a noise when dropped; color; heaviness; durability). After talking about the differences, remind students that although there is much diversity, the two items have the same worth and value.

Relate that comparison to people. Discuss ways that people are different. Ideas include some people hard to get along with vs. flexible, different colors, nationalities, size, shapes, brokeness, and so forth. Knowing what we know about the pennies and dollar, what can we say about people? All people have worth and value. Ask children to think about what that means and relate situations that you have to really remember this such as strange, old people, uncooperative family members, unfriendly friends, unfair people, disagreeable people, people from other countries. Why do you think it is so easy to judge other people so easily without knowing about them?

After discussing, hold a drawing and give the dollar bill and pennies away.

Prejudice Pledge

I pledge from this day forward to do my best to interrupt prejudice and to stop those who, because of hate, would hurt, bother or break the civil rights of anyone. I will try at all times to be aware of my own ideas against people who are different from myself. I will ask questions about cultures, religions, and races that I don't understand. I will speak out against anyone who teases, scares or actually hurts someone of a different race, religion, or group. I will reach out to support those who are targets of hate or prejudice. I will think about specific ways my school, other students and my community can support respect for people and create a prejudice-free zone. I firmly believe that one person can make a difference and that no person can be an "innocent bystander" when it comes to stopping hate.

By signing this pledge, I know that respect for individual dignity, achieving equality and opposing racism and sterotyping is the the responsibility of all people.

_____
My Signature

_____
Witness Signature

_____
Date

Date

Dear Parents,

It is not uncommon to hear the frightening stories of how prejudice and stereotyping affects our students. In Santee, California, 15-year-old Charles "Andy" Williams fired a .22 - caliber revolver at his classmates in high, killing two and wounding 13. His fellow students say the skinny, undersized freshman was often mocked and bullied by other students. Prejudice and hate persists in our society, and Santee, California joins the list of cities—Laramie, Wyoming; Jasper, Texas; Littleton, Colorado; Chicago and Los Angeles, among too many others—where violent, senseless hate crimes continue to occur.

As parents, teachers, and leaders, we must continue to teach our children to not only accept, but celebrate diversity. Intolerance is learned. Therefore, it can be unlearned. Through reading, discussion, and multicultural activities, children can better understand the value and worth of each human being and be empowered to make a difference. I once heard that you are either a part of the problem or a part of the solution. Let's agree to be part of the solution and make our world free of hate, prejudice and stereotyping. By reducing these, all people will be able to add to our world immensely making it a place of continued growth and prosperity.

If you have any questions, please feel free to contact me. A great website for more information is http://www.adl.org/adl.asp. I look forward to us growing together and making room for everyone in our community. Mother Teresa once said, "No one can do great things; only things with great love." May our love begin to transform our children's lives and flow into many generations of the future.

Sincerely,

Name

Title

La Fecha

Estimados Padres,

No es poco común escuchar historias atterradoras de como el prejuicio y la estereotipia afectan a nuestros estudiantes. En Santee, California, Charles de 15 años "Andy" Williams disparó un revolver caliber 22 a sus compañeros en la preparatoria matando a dos e hiriendo a 3. Sus compañeros dicen que el estudiante de primer año de preparatoria, pequeño y flaco era frecuentemente ridiculizado e intimidado por otros estudiantes. Odio y prejuicio persisten en nuestra sociedad, y Santee, California se une a la lista de ciudades de—Laramie, Wyoming; Jasper, Texas; Littleton, Colorado; Chicago y Los Angeles, entre muchas otras—donde crimenes violentos y sin sentido continúan ocurriendo.

Como padres, maestros, y líderes, debemos continuar enseñando a nuestros niños a no solamente aceptar, pero también celebrar la diversidad. La intolerancia se aprende. Por consiguiente, puede ser olvidada. A través de lectura, discusión, y actividades multiculturales, los niños pueden entender mejor el valor y valía de cada ser humano para poder hacer la diferencia. Una vez escuché que eres parte del problema o de la solución. Estemos de acuerdo en ser parte de la solución y hacer nuestro mundo libre de odio, prejuicio y estereotipia. Reduciendo esto, toda la gente podrá añadir inmensamente a nuestro mundo haciéndolo un lugar de continuo crecimiento y prosperidad.

Si tiene cualquier pregunta, por favor sientase libre de contactarme. Para más información esta es una gran página de internet . Espero que crezcamos juntos y hagamos lugar para todos en nuestra comunidad. La Madre Teresa dijo una vez, "Nadie puede hacer cosas grandiosas; solo cosas con gran amor." Dejemos que nuestro amor empiece a transformar la vida de nuestros niños y que fluya en muchas generaciones del futuro.

Sinceramente,

Nombre
Titulo

Appendix

"Get Real,
Get Smart,
Get Going..."
—Dr. Phil

Guidance and Counseling Needs Assessment

Por favor llene esta forma y regresela a la escuela.. Esto me ayudará a conocer a su niño mejor. ¡Gracias!

Nombre del niño _____ Cumpleaños _____ Edad_____

Nombre de los padres _____ Número de teléfono _____

Ocupación de los padres _____

❑ Ponga una marca si esta dispuesto a venir ocasionalmente a hablares a los estudiantes de su trabajo, etc.

Mi niño es bueno para _____

Mi niño necesita ayuda con _____

A mi niño le gusta _____

Académicamente, este año me gustaría ver a mi niño trabajar en _____

_____

Socialmente, me gustaría ver a mi niño trabajar en _____

_____

Mi niño necesita apoyo en las siguientes áreas
- ❑ Pesares / perdida (divorcio)
- ❑ Auto-estima
- ❑ Relaciones (amigos, padres, hermanos, maestros, etc.)
- ❑ Nuevo en la escuela
- ❑ Estudios
- ❑ Líder
- ❑ Comportamiento (siguiendo instrucciones, comportamiento violento, etc.)
- ❑ Negativismo
- ❑ La Salud (higiene, gordura, manejo de la preocupación, etc.)
- ❑ Asistencia a clases
- ❑ Introversión (pensativo, solitario)
- ❑ Valentón o intimidado
- ❑ Otros

Clases de consejero en las que le interesaría que su niño participara (Todos reciben lecciones de guía en el salón de clase)
- ❑ Grupo pequeño
- ❑ Individual
- ❑ Programas después de escuela con la consejera
- ❑ Terapia de libros

Guidance and Counseling Needs Assessment

Please complete this form about your child and send it back to school. This will help me get to know your child. Thank you!

Child's Name _____ Birthday_____Age_____

Name of Parents_____ Phone #_____

Parent's Occupation _____

❏ (Check if you would be willing to visit occasionally with students about job, and so forth.)

My child is good at _____

My child needs help with _____

My child enjoys _____

Academically, this year I would like to see my child work _____

_____

Socially, I would like to see my child work _____

_____

My child may need support in the following areas:
- ❏ Grief/loss (divorce)
- ❏ Self-esteem
- ❏ Relationships (friends, parents, siblings, step families, teachers, and so forth)
- ❏ New to School
- ❏ Academics
- ❏ Leadership
- ❏ Behavior (following directions, violent behaviors, and so forth)
- ❏ Negativity
- ❏ Health (cleanliness, obesity, stress management, and so forth)
- ❏ Attendance
- ❏ Introversion (withdrawn, lonely)
- ❏ Bullying or being bullied
- ❏ Other

Types of counseling you would be interested in your child participating (everyone receives guidance lessons in the classroom)
- ❏ Small group   Other _____
- ❏ Individual
- ❏ After school programs with counselor
- ❏ Book Therapy

Parent Opinion Inventory

1. Is your school counselor an integral part of the school community and programs?

   Es el consejero de su escuela una parte integral de la comunidad escolar y sus programas?
   - a. Yes
     Si
   - b. No
     No
   - c. Unsure
     Dudoso

2. How many times did your child participate in book club this year?

   Cuantas veces su hijo participo en el club del libro este ano?
   - a. One
     Una
   - b. Two
     Dos
   - c. All sessions
     Todas las sesiones

3. How satisfied are you with the club?

   Que tan satisfecho esta con el club?
   - a. Very satisfied
     Muy satisfecho
   - b. Satisfied
     Satisfecho
   - c. Unhappy
     Inconforme

4. Were procedures adequate for sign up and information exchange?

   Fueron los procedimientos de inscripcion y el intercambio de informacion adecuados?
   - a. Always
     Siempre
   - b. Usually
     Usualmente
   - c. Sometimes
     Algunas veces
   - d. Never
     Nunca

5. Were you well-informed and comfortable talking with the counselor?

   Estuvo bien informado y confortable hablando con el consejero?
   - a. Yes
     Si
   - b. No
     No
   - c. Sometimes
     Algunas veces

6. What is your assessment of the biblioguidance program?

   Cual es su evaluacion del programa?
   - a. Always helpful
     siempre util
   - b. Usually helpful
     usualmente util
   - c. Sometimes helpful
     algunas veces util
   - d. Never helpful
     no util

7. What is your general feeling about the way you and your child were treated in book club?

   Cual es su sentimiento general de como fueron tratados usted y su hijo en el club del libro?

8. What did you like most about book club?

   Que te gusto mas acerca del club del libro?

9. What did you like least about book club?

   Que es lo que menos te gusto del club del libro?

10. If you could make any change, what would it be?

    Si pudieras hacer caulquier cambio, Cual seria?

Student Opinion Inventory

1. Do you know who the leaders of your book club was?

    a. yes   b. no   c. unsure

2. How many times have you participated in book club this year?

    a. one   b. two   c. all sessions

3. How satisfied are you with the club?

    a. very satisfied b. satisfied   c. unhappy

4. Do you feel comfortable in the club sharing?

    a. always   b. usually   c. sometimes   d. never

5. Were the topics relevant to your life?

    a. yes   b. no   c. sometimes

6. How many things did you learn from being in book club that you can use in your life

    a. one   b. two   c. none   d. many

7. What did you like best about book club?

8. What did you like least about book club?

9. If you could make any change, what would it be?

What's the Issue?
Book-of-the-Month

I am starting a book club that will meet once a month to discuss social and emotional issues that appear in children's books. Using reading and books to help children develop socially and emotionally is a great way to enhance their development. Biblioguidance not only encourages reading, which is one of the ways to achieve academic success, but brings to light characters and situations that either work or don't work socially or emotionally. Children get a chance to dissect correct and incorrect decision-making and learn of coping skills for life's many issues through characters in books. This will be a great opportunity for your child to also interact in a small group.

This is how it will work. First, I will announce via website, bulletin board (outside my office), and monthly counselor newsletter, the book for that month's reading. It will be up to each individual to get the book from a local library or purchase the book at a book store. Second, each participating child will receive a "What's the Issue?" sheet that helps them to dissect the book socially and emotionally. The child will need to look these over in advance so that we can discuss at the meeting. Third, the child will come to the small group meeting during the last full week of the month to interact in a small group regarding the book. I will facilitate the group sessions. At each monthly meeting a drawing will be held for a "What's the Issue?" T-shirt. (Only one shirt will be given away each month from all grade levels.) ***The child must have transportation after the meeting to get home at the designated times!***

The groups will be divided up by grade levels and we will follow the following schedule:

October 20	K & 1st	3:15-3:45	November 17	3:15-3:45
October 22	2nd	3:15-3:45	November 19	3:15-3:45
October 23	3rd	3:15-3:45	November 20	3:15-3:45
October 24	4th	3:15-3:45	November 21	3:15-3:45

October's book is ***Wemberly Worried*** by Kevin Henkes. The focus of our session will be on worry and anxiety.

November's book is ***When Sophie Gets Angry*** by Molly Bang. The focus of this session will be anger.

Please return the following form if you want your child to be a part of the "What's the Issue?" club. Keep the front page for your information and return only the back side. I appreciate your support and look forward to working with your child. Please return the forms back to the child's teacher ***by October 3!***

Educationally yours,

DeDe Coffman, Counselor

By signing the following permission slip, you are agreeing to the following:

✓ Parents and child will find the book either at a local book store, library, or internet

✓ Child will read the book and look over discussion questions before book club date.

✓ Child will participate in book club by being an active listener, behaving in a way that doesn't disturb others, and interacting/sharing.

✓ Parents will notify counselor if child can't attend book club. Please try and make sure that dates are okay. Sometimes things happen, but if I get a phone call early enough, I might can add someone to the group.

✓ Parents must let teachers know either by writing a note or in person that their child is attending book club. This helps with no one missing rides!

✓ Parents will be here by 4:00 to pick up their child.

Child's Name_____Teacher _____

Parents Names _____

Address _____

Email Address _____

Phone _____

Transportation Home _____

My child_____ is allowed to participate in a small group book club, *"What's the Issue?"*, with Mrs. Coffman. I understand that it is up to me to find transportation for my child after these group sessions are over and to obtain the book for my child. I also understand that these groups will be age-appropriate for social and emotional learning. ***Put a "1" in front of the first choice and a "2" in front of the second choice!*** Groups do have cutoff numbers so get forms back quickly. You will be notified of the results of participation.

❏ October (worry) sessions

❏ November (anger) sessions

❏ Both sessions

Parent Signature _____ Date_____

Date received by counselor _____

What's the Issue?

Book-of-the-Month

Queridos Padres,

Voy a empezar un club de libros que se reunirá una vez por mes para discutir algunos de los asuntos sociales y emocionales que aparecen en los cuentos para niños. Leyendo libros para ayudar a los niños a desarrollarse social y emocionalmente es una gran manera de acrecentar su desarrollo. Biblioguidance no solo fomenta la lectura, la cual es una manera de obtener el éxito académico, pero también saca a la luz los personajes y las situaciones que funcionan o no funcionan social o emocionalmente. Los niños tienen la oportunidad de analizar minuciosamente las maneras de hacer decisiones correcta o incorrectamente y aprenden a enfrentar los problemas de la vida por medio de los personajes en los libros. Esta será una gran oportunidad para que su niño participe en un grupo pequeño.

Así es como trabajara el programa. Primero, anunciaré el libro para la lectura del mes por medio de nuestra página de Internet, la tablilla de anuncios (afuera de mi oficina), y el noticiero mensual de la consejera. Dependerá de cada individuo conseguir el libro de la biblioteca o comprarlo en la librería. Segundo, cada participante recibirá una hoja de "Lo que es el Asunto" con preguntas que les ayudarán a discernir el libro social y emocionalmente. Los niños deberán ver estas preguntas por adelantado para que puedan discutirlas en la reunión. Tercero, los niños vendrán a las reuniones de grupos pequeños durante toda la última semana del mes para discutir el libro del mes. Yo facilitare las reuniones. En cada reunión se rifará una camiseta de "Lo que es el Asunto" Solamente se rifará una camiseta por mes para todas las clases. ***Los niños deberán tener medio de trasporte después de las reuniones para que lleguen a sus casas a la hora especificada.***

Los grupos se dividirán de acuerdo al grado en que están y seguirán el siguiente programa:

Octubre 20	K & 1st	3:15–3:45	Noviembre 17	3:15-3:45
Octubre 22	2nd	3:15-3:45	Noviembre 19	3:15-3:45
Octubre 23	3rd	3:15-3:45	Noviembre 20	3:15-3:45
Octubre 24	4th	3:15-3:45	Noviembre 21	3:15-3:45

El libro para el mes de octubre será *Wemberly Worried* by Kevin Henkes. El tema de nuestra sesión será la preocupación y la ansiedad.

El libro para el mes de noviembre es *Attila the Angry* by Marjorie Weinman Sharmat. El tema de esta sesión será el enojo.

Por favor regrese la siguiente forma si quiere que su niño sea incluido en el club de "Lo que es el Asunto." Quédese con la página de enfrente para su información y regrese sólo la segunda hoja. Agradezco su apoyo y espero trabajar con su niño. Por favor regrese la forma a la maestra de su niño a más tardar el 3 de octubre.

Sinceramente,

DeDe Coffman, Counselor

Al firmar el siguiente permiso usted se compromete a lo siguiente:

✓ Los padres o el niño conseguirán el libro en la librería, la biblioteca, o por medio del Internet.

✓ El niño leerá el libro y se familiarizará con las preguntas de discusión antes de la reunión del club de libros.

✓ El niño participara en el club de libros escuchando, portándose bien, y participando / compartiendo.

✓ Los padres le avisarán a la consejera cuando su niño no pueda asistir al club de libros. Por favor asegúrese que las fechas estén bien. Hay veces que hay contratiempos, pero si me avisa con tiempo que su niño no podrá venir al club, es posible que yo pueda poner a alguien más en su lugar.

✓ Los padres le avisarán a los maestros en persona o escribiéndoles una nota que sus niños van a asistir al club de libros. Esto ayudará a que ningún niño se quede sin transporte a casa!

✓ Los padres llegarán a las 4:00 de la tarde a levantar a sus niños.

Nombre Del Niño _____ Maestra_____

Nombre De Los Padres _____

Dirección _____

Correo Electrónico _____

Numero Telefónico _____

Traslado A Casa _____

Mi niño _____ puede participar en el club de libros, "Lo que es el Asunto", Con la Señora Coffman. Yo entiendo que es mi responsabilidad proveer transportación para mi hijo después de las sesiones y de obtener los libros que mi hijo va a necesitar. También entiendo que las discusiones y temas del grupo son apropiados para el aprendizaje socio-emocional de mi niño. *¡Ponga un "1" enfrente de su primera opcion y un "2" enfrente de la segunda!* Como la admisión al club será limitada le aconsejo que regrese esta forma lo mas pronto posible. Se le notificarán los resultados de los estudiantes escogidos para participar en el club.

❏ Octubre—sesiones sobre la preocupación

❏ Noviembre—sesiones sobre el enojo.

❏ Ambas sesiones

Firma del Padre_____ Fecha _____

Fecha en que se recibió _____

What's the Issue?
Book-of-the-Month

It's time for book club sign up again! *"What's the Issue?"*—the name of the book club—was very productive last semester. Topics included anger and worry. Children were very interactive and learned some great strategies for dealing with these two emotions. In the sessions, we had discussion and sharing time as well as an activity to be involved in. The activities really reinforce the strategies and information presented. We will follow the same format for the Spring semester. *"What's the Issue?"* is a totally voluntary small group and will be limited in numbers. So, get your forms in quickly. They will be taken on a first come, first serve basis. You can find the topics and times below. These may change after the January sessions depending on numbers per grade level. Before signing up, please read the instructions so that we can make sure to run this program successfully and efficiently.

Please return the following form if you want your child to be a part of the *"What's the Issue?"* club. Keep the front page for your information and return only the back side. I appreciate your support and look forward to working with your child. If you have any questions, please let me know. Please return the forms back to the child's teacher **by January 9th**.

Educationally yours,

DeDe Coffman, Counselor

January 26, February 23, April 19	Kindergarten
January 28, February 25, April 21	1st
January 29, February 26, April 22	2nd
January 30, February 27, April 23	3rd & 4th

January's book is *Amazing Grace* by Mary Hoffman. Session focus: goal-setting

February's book is *The Thingumajig Book of Manners* by Irene Keller. Focus: manners

April's book is *The Grouchy Ladybug* by Eric Carle. Session focus: friendships

By signing the following permission slip, you are agreeing to the following:

✓ Parents and child will find the book either at a local book store, library or internet.

✓ Child will read the book and look over discussion questions before book club date.

✓ Child will participate in book club by being an active listener, behaving in a way that doesn't disturb others, and interacting/sharing.

✓ Parents will notify counselor if child can't attend book club. Please try and make sure that dates are okay. Sometimes things happen, but if I get a phone call early enough, I might can add someone to the group.

✓ Parents must let teachers know either by writing a note or in person that their child is attending book club. This helps with no one missing rides!

✓ Parents will be here by 4:00 to pick up their child.

Child's Name_____Teacher _____

Parents Names _____

Address _____

Email Address _____

Phone _____

Transportation Home _____

My child_____ is allowed to participate in a small group book club, *"What's the Issue?"*, with Mrs. Coffman. I understand that it is up to me to find transportation for my child after these group sessions are over and to obtain the book for my child. I also understand that these groups will be age-appropriate for social and emotional learning. ***Put a "1" in front of the first choice and a "2" in front of the second choice!*** Groups do have cutoff numbers so get forms back quickly. You will be notified of the results of participation.

❏ January (goal-setting) book club

❏ February (manners) book club

❏ April (friendship) book club

❏ All sessions

Parent Signature _____ Date_____

Date received by counselor _____

What's the Issue?

Book-of-the-Month

    ¡Otra vez es tiempo para inscribirse en el club del libro! "¿Cuál es el problema?", el cual es el nombre del club del libro, el semester pasado fue muy productivo. Los temas incluyeron ira y preocupación. Los niños interactuaron bastante y aprendieron algunasestupendas estrategias para enfrentarse con estas emociones. En las sesiones, tuvimos tiempos de discusión e intercambio así como actividades también. Las actividades refuerzan las estrategias e información presentada. Seguiremos el mismo formato para el semester de primavera. "¿Cuál es el problema?" es un pequeño grupo totalmente voluntario y tendrá cupo limitado. Así que entregue sus formas rápidamente. Serán recogidas de acuerdo como lleguen, las primeras se servirán primero. A continuación puede encontrar los horarios y tópicos. Estos pueden cambiar después de las sesiones de enero dependiendo en los números por nivel de grado. Antes de inscribirse, por favor lea las instrucciones para que podamos estar seguro de que el programa sea eficiente y exitoso.

    Por favor regrese la siguiente forma si quiere que su hijo participe en el club "¿Cuál es el problema?" Para su información quédese con la página frontal y regrese aolamente la parte trasera. Agradezco su apoyo y espero trabajar con su hijo. Si tiene alguna pregunta, por favor dejeme saber. Regrese las formas a la maestro de su hijo *Para el 9 de enero*.

Educacionalmente suya,

DeDe Coffman, Consejera

26 de enero, 23 de febrero, 19 de abril Kindergarten

28 de enero, 25 de febrero, 21 de abril 1st

29 de enero, 26 de febrero, 22 de abril 2nd

30 de enero, 27 de febrero, 23 de abril 3rd & 4th

    El libro de enero es *Amazing Grace* por Mary Hoffman. Tema de la sesión: estableciendo metas

    El libro de febrero es *The Thingumajig Book of Manners* por Irene Keller. **TEMA:** modales

    El libro de abril es *The Grouchy Ladybug* por Eric Carle. Tema de la sesión: amistades

Al firmar el siguiente permiso, usted está de acuerdo con lo siguiente:

✓ Padres e hijos encontrarán el libro ya sea en una bibliioteca, librería o el internet

✓ El niño leerá el libro y verá las preguntas de discussion antes de la junta del club.

✓ El niño participará en el club del libro siendo un oyente activo, comportandose de una manera que no moleste a otros, e interactuando/compartiendo.

✓ Los padres notificarán a la consejera si el niño no puede asistir al club. Por favor esté seguro de que las fechas están bien. Algunas veces cosas suceden, pero si se me notifica con sufuciente anticipación, puedo añadir alguien más al grupo.

✓ Los padres deben decirle a las maestros ya sea por escrito o en persona que su hijo está asistiendo al club del libro. ¡Esto ayuda a que nadie pierda su regreso!

✓ Los padres estarán aquí para recoger a su hijo a las 4:00.

Nombre Del Niño _____ Maestra_____

Nombre De Los Padres _____

Dirección _____

Correo Electrónico _____

Numero Telefónico _____

Traslado A Casa _____

Mi niño _____ puede participar en el club de libros, "Lo que es el Asunto", Con la Señora Coffman. Yo entiendo que es mi responsabilidad proveer transportación para mi hijo después de las sesiones y de obtener los libros que mi hijo va a necesitar. También entiendo que las discusiones y temas del grupo son apropiados para el aprendizaje socio-emocional de mi niño. *¡Ponga un "1" enfrente de su primera opcion y un "2" enfrente de la segunda!* Como la admisión al club será limitada le aconsejo que regrese esta forma lo mas pronto posible. Se le notificarán los resultados de los estudiantes escogidos para participar en el club.

❑ enero (establecer las metas) del club del libro

❑ febrero (modales) del club del libro

❑ abril (amistad) club del libro

❑ Todas las sesiones

Firma del Padre_____fecha_____

Fecha recibida por la consejera _____

What's the Issue?

Dear _____.

You made it! Book Club will meet the last week of the month, and I want you there. Don't forget to go over your discussion page with Mom and Dad. Bring your book with you if possible and a winning attitude! See you soon!

_____

(Counselor's Name)

Group Attendance

Student	Teacher	1	2	3	4	5	6

Session Topics
1.
2.
3.
4.
5.

Biblioguidance Book List

TITLE	AUTHOR	ISSUE
201 Icebreakers	West	
A Big Fat Enormous Lie	Marjorie Sharmat	lying, honesty
A House for Hermit Crab	Eric Carle	needs
A Simple Path	Mother Teresa	love
Adam and Eve—Pinch Me	Johnston	
Alexander and the Day	Judith Viorst	bad days
Alexandra Keeper of the Dreams	Mary Baumgartner	resiliency, strg.
Amazing Grace	Mary Hoffman	goal-setting
And the Winner Is	LL Cool J	sportsmanship
Arnie the Doughnut	Laurie Keller	self-discovery
Attila the Angry	Marjorie Sharmat	anger
Authentic Happiness	Martin Seligman	happiness
Bartholomew Bossy	Marjorie Sharmat	bossiness
Blabber Mouse	True Kelley	blabbering
Book of Mean People	Morrison	anger/mean
Brand New Kid	Katie Couric	bullying
Bringing Up Boys	James Dobson	parenting boys
Bringing Up Kids Without Tearing..	Kevin Leman	parenting
Cat's Got Your Tongue	Charles Schaefer	shyness
Cheating Lessons	Cappo	cheating
Children's Literature	M. Rudman	
Christopher, Will you Please Clean	Itah Sadu	responsibility
Chrysanthemum	Kevin Henkes	teasing
Cinder Edna	Ellen Jackson	uniqueness
Cliques	Giannetti	parenting strat.
Courage	Waber	courage
Crickwing	Cannon	bullying
Dare to Win	Canfield	overcome
Dinosaurs Divorce (series)	Laurene Krasny	divorce
Dirty Bertie	David Roberts	bad habits
Don't Laugh at Me	Steve Seskin	bully, tolerance
Eaglet's World	Minshull	development
Elmer	David McKee	individuality
Emotional Intelligence	Goleman	emotional iq
English Roses	MaDonna	cliques, friends
Franklin and the Thunderstorm	Paulette Bourgeois	worry
Frederick	Lionni	dreams

Friends of a Feather	Bill Cosby	being oneself
Frizzy the Fearful	Marjorie Sharmat	fear
Giant King	Kathleen Pelley	expectations
Girl Wars	Dellasega	girl strate.
Grouchy Lady Bug	Eric Carle	grouchiness
Grumley the Grouchy	Marjorie Sharmat	grouchiness
Hey Little Ant	Hoose	bullying
Hooway for Wodney Wat	Helen Lester	bullying
Hooway for Wodney Wat	Helen Lester	uniqueness
How are you Peeling	Saxton Freymann	feelings
How Could you Do That	Laura Schlessinger	responsibility
How Santa Go His Job	Stephen Krensky	career choice
How to Lose All Your Friends	Nancy Carlson	friendship
How to Win and Influence Friends	Carnegie	influence
Humpty Dumpty Eggslodes	Kevin O'Malley	anger
I Knew You Could	Dorfman	self esteem
I'm Gonna Like Me	Jamie Lee Curtis	self esteem
I'm Like You, You're Like Me	Gainer	prejudice
It's Hard to Be 5	Jamie Lee Curtis	Kindgart.
It's Not My Fault	Nancy Carlson	responsibility
Jag	LeeAnn Rimes	worry/peers
Jeremy's Decision	Ardyth Brott	careers
Jungle Drums	Graeme Base	inner beauty
Just the Two of Us	Will Smith	father relation
Just the Way You Are	Marcus Pfister	self esteem
Leo the Late Bloomer	Robert Kraus	late bloomers
Leo the Late Bloomer	Robert Kraus	patience
Liar Liar Pants on Fire	Diane DeGroat	honesty
Life Happens	McCoy	relationships
Lilly's Purple Plastic Purse	Kevin Henkes	anger
Little Flower	Gloria Rand	determination
Little Red	Sarah Ferguson	courage
Living, Loving and Learning	Leo Buscaglia	living
Lucretia the Unbearable	Marjorie Sharmat	selfishness
Mean Chicks, Cliques, and Dirty	Erika Karres	girl bullying
Miss Nelson is Missing	H. Allard	appreciation
Mr. Peabodies Apples	MaDonna	power of word
My Brother is from Outer Space	Vivian Ostrow	siblings
My Many Colored Days	Dr. Seuss	moods
My Penguin Osbert	Elizabeth Kimmel	wise choices

Odd Girl Out	Rachel Simmons	girl bullying
Oh, The Places I'll Go	Dr. Seuss	dreams, goals
Old Turtle	Douglas Wood	inner peace
Oliver Button is a Sissy	DePaola	bullying
One Candle	Eve Bunting	pesever./hope
Ophelia....	Mary Pipher	girl issues
Peeling the Onion	Orr	perseverance
Penny Lee and her TV	Glenn McCoy	TV too much
Picky Mrs. Pickle	Christine Schneider	pickiness
Positive Coaching	Thompson	coaching
Putting Your Family First	Doherty	overscheduled
Queen Bees and Wannabees	Rosalinda Wiseman	girls and cliques
Rainbow Fish and Blue Whale	Marcus Pfister	worry
Rainbow Fish and the Big Whale	Marcus Pfister	worry
Rainbow Fish to the Rescue	Marcus Pfister	prejudice
Real Boys	William Pollack	parenting boys
Recess Queen	Alexis O'Neill	girls' bullying
Road Less Traveled	Peck	relationships
Rude Mule	Edwards/Nascimberi	manners
Salt in His Shoes	Deloris Jordan	dreams
Santa Kid	James Patterson	believing
Seeds of Greatness	Waitley	
Sensitive Issues:	Rasinski	
Seven Steps to Help Your Child Worry Less	Goldstein	worry strate.
Sneetches	Dr. Seuss	prejudice
Spider and the Fly	Tony Diterlizzi	deceptiveness
Stand Tall, Molly Lou	Patty Lovell	confidence
Stellaluna	Janell Cannon	masking
Tacky in Trouble	Helen Lester	mischief
Taking Back Your Kids	Doherty	parenting
Taking Back Your Marriage	Doherty	marriage
Tear Soup	Pat Schwiebert	grief
The Ant Bully	Nickle	bullying
The Bunyans	Audrey Wood	
The Clic	Lisa Harrison	cliques
The Colors of Us	Katz	prejudice
The Cow that Went Oink	Bernard Most	uniqueness
The Crayon Box	DeRolf	equality
The Difference a Daddy Makes	Kevin Leman	father
The Fall of Freddie Leaf	Leo Buscaglia	grief

The First Starry Night	Joan Isom	friendship
The Giving Tree	Shell Silvetstein	grateful
The Hurt	T. Poleski	grief
The Kissing Hand	Audrey Penn	Kindgart. fear
The Little Baby Snoogle-Flejeer	Jimmy Carter	individuality
The Lovables in the Kingdom of SE	Diane Loomeras	self-esteem
The Man Who Walked Between Towers	Mordicai Gerstein	courage/fear
The Other Side of the Fence	Woodson	prejudice
The Pinkish, Purplish Bluish Egg	Bill Peet	prejudice
The Terrible Fight	Sharon St. Germain	fighting
The Very Lonely Firefly	Eric Carle	friendship
Thingamujig Book of Manners	Irene Keller	manners
Tomorrow Maybe	James	growing up
True Story of Three Pigs	Jon Scieszka	perspective
Truffle's Christmas	Anna Currey	unselfishness
Uncle Willy and Soup	DyAnne DiSalvo Ryan	helping others
Wemberly Worried	Kevin Henkes	worry
What Are You So Grumpy About	Tom Lichtenheld	grouchy
What Do you Say Dear	Sesyle Joslin	ver. manners
What's the Recipe for Friends	Greg Williamson	friends
What's Wrong with Timmy	Maria Shriver	differences
When 1st Grade Takes a Test	M. Cohen	test anxiety
When Sophie Gets Angry	Molly Bang	anger
Whoever you Are	Fox	self esteem
Why Mosquitoes Buzz	Leo Dillon	anger
Willy the Champ	Browne	bullying
Won't You Ever Listen	Carol Cummings	listening
Zinnia and Dot	Lisa Ernst	competition

DeDe Coffman